THE TRUTH ABOUT THE COMING GLOBAL CURRENCY RESET

By Marcus Curtis

Master edition 2016

© Copyright 2014, 2nd edition 2016 Marcus Curtis

ISBN 9781520291352

All rights reserved. No part of this book may be used or reproduced in any manner whatsoever without prior written permission from the author/publisher.
Edition License Notes

This book details a number of events that happened throughout history. It also gives financial data found throughout different periods of time. The analysis of these events and the meaning of the financial data found in this book is strictly the opinion of the author. His views reflect his own personal research.

Table of Contents

Chapter One - What Is The Global Currency Reset?.. 5
Chapter Two - Early Monetary History........ 11
    The Debasement of Roman Coins.......... 15
    The Rise of Currency............................ 16
    Fiat Money... 18
Chapter Three - America's Forgotten Monetary History.. 19
    Every American should know................ 20
Chapter Four - New Federal Money Laws.. 27
    My Observations................................. 38
    Rewriting History For The GCR Agenda.. 41
Chapter Five - The Global Economy Emerges 47
    International Monetary Fund (IMF) 50
    International Bank for Reconstruction and Development (IBRD) 51
    Bretton Woods System......................... 51
    General Agreement on Tariffs and Trade (GATT) 52
    The Petro Dollar 53
    The Trilateral Commission.................... 57
Chapter Six - Simple Money Mechanics 59
    Inflation... 59
    Hyperinflation 63
    Money Creation and the Federal Reserve 64
    Fractional Reserve Banking 66
    Money Stock 67
    Expansion and contraction of the Money Supply 69
    Revaluation and Devaluation 71
    Keynesian Economics 72
    The Federal Reserve 76
    BRICS and PIIGS 84

BRICS 84
PIIGS 84
Derivatives 85
Chapter Seven - The 2008 Meltdown 87
A Securitization food chain linked everything together 90
Government's Role 93
The dollar is the world's currency reserve. 100
Chapter Eight - Iraq and the Dinar 102
Chapter Nine - The Aftermath 111
The Mechanics of an overnight dollar crash 122
Chapter Ten - The Origins Of The Global Currency Reset 127
The Coming Dollar Crash 130
Chapter Eleven - Problems Associated With a Reset 134
Chapter Twelve - Don't Believe the Hype 146
China 146
Iraq 150
Religious Point of View 150
Buzz Words 151
Fiat Currency 151
Linear Thinking 153
Fractional Reserve Banking 154
The IMF 155
The Truth Is 156
Chapter Thirteen - The Final Analysis 157
The Sales Pitch 164
Chapter Fourteen - Trust But Verify 170
About The Author 179

Chapter One - What Is The Global Currency Reset?

In the 20th century a global economy emerged; an economy ruled by the U.S. dollar. Some nations used the dollar exclusively as their main currency. Other nations became dollarized, having two currencies in circulation. The United States Dollar (USD) was the global currency king.

Toward the end of the century and into the new millennium the economic landscape began to change. A major economic meltdown happened in 2008. A crash of the U.S. economy was felt around the world. A lot of wealth vanished into thin air due to reduced values in the housing market. Trillions of dollars in debt were erased from the books. Millions of people fell below the poverty line, and millions became unemployed. This triggered a meltdown of the world's economy.

The United States government was very concerned about deflation, so it began to buy toxic assets in a program known as TARP (Troubled Asset Relief Program). By March 2009, it held $1.75 trillion of bank debt and mortgage-backed securities. This action led to the release of more dollars into the world.

Government debt reached well above $9 trillion by the end of 2008, and the Federal Reserve began flooding the global financial system with even more dollars. Speculation at the time was that all of this would serve to weaken the dollar further. The Federal Reserve started the Quantitative Easing program, (also known as "QE") in November of 2008.

QE was implemented by buying specified amounts of financial assets from commercial banks and other private institutions. This raised the price of those financial assets and lowered their yield, while simultaneously increasing the total money supply (or "monetary base"). That allowed even more USD into circulation.

It only took seven months for the national debt to increase from $13 trillion on June 1, 2010 to $14 trillion on December 31 of the same year. At the time of this writing we are reaching a national debt of close to $20 trillion as we near the end of Obama's administration. Many of these events only served to cause speculation about the dollar's future as the dollar supply grows year after year.

Currency wars broke out because of these events. Countries began competing with each other to attain a low exchange rate for their respective currencies. As the price to buy a particular currency falls, the real price of exports from that country also falls. That brings jobs and a strong economy to nations that have a low exchange rate. Imports become more expensive as a country's currency falls in value on the foreign exchange. Artificially low exchange rates placed on any currency act as a hidden tariff on imports. As the USD started to fall around the world due to the 2008 meltdown and the perceived outcome of the Federal Reserve's policies, it concerned many nations because that would potentially have a direct impact on their economies. In 2011 Vladimir Putin said *"If over there (in America) there is a systemic malfunction. This will affect everyone. They are living like parasites off the global economy and their monopoly of the dollar."*

Russia and China agreed to start trading with each other using their own currencies, and started limiting exchanges using the dollar. China and other nations called for a new international currency to replace the dollar. Some countries wanted SDRs (Special Drawing Rights - foreign exchange reserve assets maintained by the International Monetary Fund) used as a new international currency. The IMF allocated SDRs. China became accepted into the basket of currencies on October 1st 2016. Even though this move was coming for a while, many conspiracy theories predict that this one event will put an end to the dollar on a global level.

So now, it seems as though the USD is in danger of losing its spot as the reserve currency for the world. There is talk of a Global Currency Reset. The rumors are running wild. The theory is that all currencies will reset in value, including the dollar. The USD will be forsaken as a reserve currency as the world begins to move toward a basket of currencies as the new reserve system.

Some people that represent gold and silver merchants talk about different scenarios that make up a coming global currency reset (or "GCR"). Currency dealers also talk about the anticipated GCR event. Some speculate that a nation's currency will be valued by the raw resources that can be found in that nation. The more resources the nation has, the higher the currency value for that nation.

These rumors only serve to bring about fear, and cause people to seek a safe place to put their wealth. Some look to assets, some look to foreign currencies, and some look to precious metals like silver and gold. Many doomsday naysayers have surfaced, proclaiming an end to the almighty dollar. Some predict the end to the American economy and the American way of life.

Many conspiracy theories about money and the history of money rise and grow stronger. The internet quickly fills with them. Television advertisements appear declaring the dollar will collapse. There is a growing belief held by many people that the dollar will crash overnight, and new converts to this belief are being made all the time! These fears really seemed more plausible after the 2008 global meltdown.

These people use fancy terms like "global currency reset", "fiat currency", "fractional reserve banking", and "linear thinking". Some say that we are about to witness a transfer of wealth and value out of the U.S. dollar and into other more tangible assets. Some professing Christians claim that this coming GCR event is part of biblical prophecy. This GCR idea has spawned groups of people who have become preppers. Sales from emergency food supplies, precious metals, foreign currencies, newsletters, and other doomsday merchandise have now become big business!

All of this raises a few questions. What is the truth concerning this global currency reset? How did the United States get into this mess? What does the future actually hold for the world's economy? What parts of this global currency reset are based on wild conspiracy theory and what parts are true? Will the dollar really collapse in one night? What changes are coming to the global economy?

In order to address these questions we must first learn a little bit about economics. We need to learn about how money actually works. I will make you this promise. We will not be bogged down with advanced equations and mathematical problems normally found in the study of economics. Not only will this put you to sleep, but it will cause you to miss the solutions that are found in an overall understanding of how the economy really works. Instead, we'll discover the hidden agendas found from people who financed the main economic events throughout history. We will develop a layman's understanding as to how money actually works as we lay out an overview of the global economy.

We can also gain an understanding of this global process by looking at history; monetary history in particular. It has been said that those who do not know history are doomed to repeat it. I say that those who know history are doomed to watch those who do not know history repeat it, and because the people who know history are in the minority, they will repeat it too. Therefore, it is better to prepare for it. We'll soon discover that everyone has agendas and self-serving motives.

We will find that this global currency reset is actually a story that is intriguing, and filled with mystery and suspense. Like many conspiracy theories, this plot will keep you on the edge of your seat! So join me as we follow the money and find the answers to the questions regarding the GCR. We will start with monetary history. This will lay the foundation for everything that follows.

It is the goal of this book to provide the truth regarding the global currency reset. We will debunk all of the conspiracy theories that have been attached to this belief system, many of which attempt to rewrite history. This is why we need to start by studying history. Learning the real history behind an event will enable you to spot many of the false claims and false narratives. As we study real global economics and as we see how money really works, you will discover that many aspects of this GCR theory can be disproven.

The last chapter of the book contains a multitude of links and references that will allow you to do your own research. Don't just accept my conclusions when you reach the end of this book. Do your own follow up analysis! The last chapter will help you get started and point you in a few different directions.

Chapter Two - Early Monetary History

Money in its most basic function is a medium of exchange, and declares the value that is placed upon goods, services, and labor. It is used to allow people to acquire the things they may need or want, while the recipients accept this medium of exchange because they can use it to obtain the things they may need and want in the future.

Where did money come from? Well, before the use of money bartering was used to exchange goods. People traded the things they had for things they wanted. If someone made baskets, then they could take those baskets and trade them for food, spears, or even arrows. But often there were times when the barter system was unfair, depending on what the person needed. If you wanted an apple but the only thing you had to trade was a horse, then that presented a huge problem. So a more sophisticated means of exchange was needed.

Over the years there were many things that were used as money. Indians used beads and shells. I have read about some cultures that even used salt as a form of money. Perhaps the oldest form of money is gold and silver, both of which were used in ancient Egypt. It may even amaze some people to learn that the use of silver was recorded in the Bible, the earliest reference being when Abraham wanted to bury his wife Sara.

Gen 23:3 And Abraham rose up from before his dead and said to the Hittites,

Gen 23:4 "I am a sojourner and foreigner among you; give me property among you for a burying place, that I may bury my dead out of my sight."

Gen 23:5 The Hittites answered Abraham,

Gen 23:6 "Hear us, my lord; you are a prince of God among us. Bury your dead in the choicest of our tombs. None of us will withhold from you his tomb to hinder you from burying your dead."

Gen 23:7 Abraham rose and bowed to the Hittites, the people of the land.

Gen 23:8 And he said to them, "If you are willing that I should bury my dead out of my sight, hear me and entreat for me Ephron the son of Zohar,

Gen 23:9 that he may give me the cave of Machpelah, which he owns; it is at the end of his field. For the full price let him give it to me in your presence as property for a burying place."

Gen 23:10 Now Ephron was sitting among the Hittites, and Ephron the Hittite answered Abraham in the hearing of the Hittites, of all who went in at the gate of his city,

Gen 23:11 "No, my lord, hear me: I give you the field, and I give you the cave that is in it. In the sight of the sons of my people I give it to you. Bury your dead."

Gen 23:12 Then Abraham bowed down before the people of the land.

Gen 23:13 And he said to Ephron in the hearing of the people of the land, "But if you will, hear me: I give the price of the field. Accept it from me, that I may bury my dead there."

Gen 23:14 Ephron answered Abraham,

Gen 23:15 "My lord, listen to me: a piece of land worth four hundred shekels of silver, what is that between you and me? Bury your dead."

Gen 23:16 Abraham listened to Ephron, and Abraham weighed out for Ephron the silver that he had named in the hearing of the Hittites, four hundred shekels of silver, according to the weights current among the merchants. -ESV

    A shekel at that time was a unit of weight. When metals were used for money in Abraham's day, scales were used. The unit of weight in this case was a shekel. When Egypt used gold and silver as money they also used scales to weigh the metals. The price of goods had to be weighed out in every transaction.
    According to the Greek historian Herodotus, writing in the fifth century BC, the Lydian people were the first people to have used gold and silver coinage, but the actual truth is the earliest coins are found mainly in the parts of modern Turkey that formed only part of the ancient kingdom of Lydia. These coins were first produced in the seventh century BC, and only had a design on one side.
    Since the exact unit of weight was in the coin itself, scales were no longer needed. Their earlier coins were a mixture of other metals, but in time Lydia separated the metals and made silver and gold coins. These coins were eventually made from a naturally occurring mixture of gold and silver called "electrum". The shekel later came to refer to a coin used in Israel that weighed …. you guessed it … **one shekel!**
    Coins as an invention eventually made their way to Athens, and they exploded in use. Athenian coins can be found dating back to the late 5th and early 4th centuries BC. Athens was one of the first societies to have a tax system and free commerce. Their prosperity allowed them to build huge temples and create massive works of art, along with many public works projects.

When Athens fought in the Peloponnesian war everything changed. They had monetary problems because of the war when they lost access to their gold and silver mines. They were sending money to their soldiers who were many miles away and marching on foot. That enabled them to buy supplies and receive services from the local populations, but it also created a shortage of money in the city of Athens. As a result they began to experience deflation as more and more money was exported. They started to debase their coins by taking coins generated from their tax revenues and melting them down to mix with copper. People took those coins at face value until there were too many of them in circulation.

Then something called "Gresham's Law" kicked in. Gresham's Law simply states that people will spend the money that is common first, and they will save the rare money and spend it last. Because the debased coins became common and the gold and silver coins became rare, the people saved those coins and only spent the debased coins. Gold and silver coins began to dry up.

Suddenly it took a lot of copper coins to buy some of those rare gold and silver coins that were minted in Athens before the war! This was a large factor in Athens' downfall. In 404 BC Athens surrendered to Sparta, and it was the debasing of the money supply combined with the expense of war and public works that finally brought them down.

The Debasement of Roman Coins

Inflation happened during the Roman era as well. This period of inflation was during the time of Nero all the way up to the crisis of the 3rd century. Roman coins used to be pure silver, but Rome began to mix other metals with their silver coins in order to increase their money supply. Coinage in the Late Roman Period suffered from severe debasement. By 250 AD the amount of the silver on the coin had been reduced to just 5 percent.

For the production of these "silver" coins a base of copper, tin, and lead-alloys was used. To complete the process the coin was overlaid with silver. The surface was covered by thin silver plating, which wore off easily during the circulation of the coins. Much to the surprise of the Romans, the extra coin supply brought inflation to the Roman Empire. As more of these debased coins entered circulation they stole value from the coins that were already in circulation, causing inflation for the Roman Empire. Let's look at the progression of the debasement leading up to the crisis of the 3rd century. We will look at it this way: Emperor – Reign - Average Silver Content.

Nero - 54 to 68 AD - 91.80%
Galba - 68 to 69 AD - 92.60%
Otho - 69 AD - 98.20%
Vitellius - 69 AD - 86.10%
Vespasian - 69 to 79 AD - 84.90%
Titus - 79 to 81 AD - 80.30%
Domitian - 81 to 96 AD - 90.80%
Nerva - 96 to 98 AD - 90.70%
Trajan - 98 to 117 AD - 85.40%

Hadrian - 117 to 138 AD - 84.10%
Antoninus Pius - 138 to 161 AD - 80.00%
Marcus Aurelius - 161 to 180 AD - 76.20%
Commodus - 180 to 192 AD - 72.20%
Pertinax - 193 AD - 76.00%
Didius Julianus - 193 AD - 81.00%
Septimius Severus -193 to 211 AD - 58.30%

During the crisis of the third century Rome was struggling for its very existence. They almost collapsed as a nation. Their silver content per coin was so low and the money supply expanded so much that inflation became a major issue. The more coins in circulation, the less they were worth. (Source = Sture Bolin's *"State Currency in the Roman Empire to 300 AD"* - 1958)

"The budget should be balanced, the treasury should be refilled, public debt should be reduced, the arrogance of officialdom should be tempered and controlled, and the assistance of foreign lands should be curtailed lest the republic becomes bankrupt. People must again learn to work, instead of living on public assistance." – Marcus Tullius Cicero, 55 BC (Source = Societe Generale Tulane University)

The Rise of Currency

The use of coinage gave rise to goldsmiths; people who purified gold and certified its purity. They lent out this gold and charged interest. The goldsmiths developed large vaults to store the gold. As a result, other people wanted to secure their gold so they rented space from the goldsmiths where they could store it. The goldsmiths would then issue paper receipts for that gold. In time people began trading the paper receipts instead of going to get the gold to pay their debt. The paper receipts that represented the gold became known as currency. They were nothing but a mere claim check or a receipt to indicate the amount of gold that was on deposit.

Eventually the goldsmiths realized that people were exchanging these receipts instead of redeeming the gold, so they created more receipts without the gold to back the new receipts. They introduced those new receipts into the economy for their own personal gain. When people inevitably figured out what the goldsmiths were doing, a mob usually showed up at their places of business with the intention of getting their gold back. Needless to say, a run on the goldsmith was not good for his business.

This type of money is called representative money because it simply represents a claim on an asset such as gold or silver. Commodity money is created from an asset such as precious metals like gold or silver. These assets are made into coins that are then used as a medium of exchange.

The goldsmith business slowly evolved into the modern banking system we see today. In our modern banking system our money is based on assets like gold and silver, and other assets like treasury bonds. Debt is also monetized, and it is circulated as money throughout the economy. This system has slowly evolved over the last 300 years.

Fiat Money

Fiat money is a currency established as money by government regulation or law. It is established in the sense of an order or decree. The first use of fiat money was recorded in China around 1000 AD, and its use became widespread during the Yuan and Ming dynasties. Since then it has been used by various countries around the world. Fiat money has been defined as "all money declared by a government to be legal tender", "government-issued money which is neither convertible by law to any other thing, nor fixed in value in terms of any objective standard", and "intrinsically valueless money or money that has no value outside of government decree".

Chapter Three - America's Forgotten Monetary History

Today, most Americans do not understand what a central bank is or what function it has. Americans are no longer being taught economics, and they no longer learn the history of America's central banks. These things are being ignored in our classrooms, and as a society we have been dumbed down about the origins of central banks, monetary legislation, or even how money works.

The truth is, the debate over central banks is one of the most important themes in U.S. history. America has had three central banks in its history. Our current central bank is called "The Federal Reserve", and it is a part of our federal government. Many people claim that it is really a private bank, and in this case "Federal" is just a title that is put together with "Reserve" to make you think it is a part of our government.

The truth is our nation was birthed in the midst of a conflict over taxation and the control of our money through something called "The Stamp Act". A central banking system has played a major part in nearly all of the wars that America has fought. Presidents that resisted the central bankers were persecuted and shot, while other presidents were endorsed by these same banks.

In this day and age, we as Americans are taught a sanitized version of American history. This history omits the role of the central banks and what their purpose was. Money history is lumped together with economics, and it has become a very boring subject that uses numbers, figures, and equations that have the cumulative effect of taking a sleeping pill.

If you want to know what really happened and how the central banking system shaped our history, then just follow the money. Real history is not only found in the events that happened, but also in learning about the people who bankrolled those events and the agenda they had at the time. What should we all know about America's money history? Here is a list of 66 interesting facts or events behind the evolution of money and the monetary laws that shaped America.

Every American should know....

1. The very first central banks were set up in Europe. These central banks were private banks, and they were given control of the nation's money supply wherever they were set up.

2. England was at war with France from 1756 to 1763. As a result of The Seven Years' War with France, King George III of England was deeply in debt to the central bankers of England.

3. In an attempt to raise revenue and pay off debt, King George tried to tax the colonies in America. He did this through The Stamp Act. He felt that since part of his debt came from defending the colonies due to the Seven Years' War, then the colonies should share in the debt incurred from that war. Of course, the colonies did not agree.

4. Benjamin Franklin went before the Parliament in London in 1763. One of the topics discussed was America's economy.

5. The Currency Act of 1764 ordered the American colonists to stop printing their own money. Colonial script was the money the colonists were using at this time. It was to be exchanged at a two-to-one ratio for "notes" from the Bank of England. This was England's way of taxing America

6. When asked why the American colonies had lost respect for Parliament, Benjamin Franklin said:

"To a concurrence of causes: the restraints lately laid on their trade, by which the bringing of foreign gold and silver into the Colonies was prevented; the prohibition of making paper money among themselves, and then demanding a new and heavy tax by stamps; taking away, at the same time, trials by juries, and refusing to receive and hear their humble petitions."

7. Around the time of Adam Smith (1723-1790) there was a massive growth in the banking industry. Within the new system of ownership and investment, money holders were able to reduce the state's intervention in economic affairs, remove barriers to competition, and in general allow anyone willing to work hard enough and who also had access to capital to become a capitalist. It was not until over 100 years after Adam Smith however that U.S. companies began to apply his policies to a large scale, and shift the balance of financial power from England to America.

8. The house of Rothschild was established in 1776 in Frankfurt, Germany. It is widely believed that this dynasty had a major impact on the first two central banks, but they became a dominant force in the 19th century.

9. The Continental Congress was desperate for funds, and met at Independence Hall. They appointed Robert Morris (an arms dealer) to head the Bank of North America, which was to be closely modeled after the Bank of England (a central bank). The charter of the Bank of North America called for private investors to put up $400,000 capital as the initial investment, but when Robert Morris was unable to raise the capital he used his political influence to have gold that was loaned to America by France to be deposited in the new bank. Then he loaned this money to himself and his friends to "reinvest" in shares of the bank.

The bank held a monopoly over the national currency from the period of 1781-1785. The value of American currency dropped, and the bank's charter was not renewed. The first attempt at a central banking system had failed. The effort to kill the Bank of North America was led by William Findley.

10. William Findley later commented:

"The institution, having no principle but that of avarice, will never be varied in its object ... to engross all the wealth, power and influence of the state".

Now you see the mission of every central bank in that era. This is what central banks did. It is interesting to note that Alexander Hamilton endorsed the Bank of North America.

11. Gouverneur Morris of Pennsylvania was one of the authors of the U.S. Constitution. He solemnly warned us in 1787 that we must not allow the bankers to enslave us.

"The rich will strive to establish their dominion and enslave the rest. They always did. They always will... They will have the same effect here as elsewhere, if we do not, by the power of government, keep them in their proper spheres."

12. After the attempt to establish a central bank in the 1780s had failed, the First Bank of the United States was established in 1791.

Alexander Hamilton cut a deal with the South. He said that he would support the move of the nation's capital to Washington D.C. in exchange for Southern support for the establishment of a central bank. Once again, this was a private bank. It was America's first central bank.

13. George Washington signed the bill creating the First Bank of the United States on April 25, 1791. It was given a 20-year charter. Alexander Hamilton was our nation's treasurer at this time. He pushed for the passage of the central bank. James Madison opposed it, and led an attempt to block the bank. He said:

"History records that the money changers have used every form of abuse, intrigue, deceit, and violent means possible to maintain their control over governments by controlling money and its issuance."

14. There was a tax placed on liquor to finance the first central bank and provide a way for the newly formed federal government to pay its debt. A rebellion broke out in Pennsylvania to protest the new tax, and became known as "The Whiskey Rebellion". At this time the national capital (Philadelphia) was located in the same state were this rebellion broke out. On his own initiative, Hamilton drafted a presidential proclamation denouncing resistance to the excise laws. Washington signed the proclamation on September 15, 1792. It was then published and printed in many newspapers.

15. In the first five years of the First Bank of the United States, the U.S. government borrowed $8.2 million. Because new money went into circulation due to this lending, the inflation rate rose to 72%.

16. In 1798, Thomas Jefferson said:

"I wish it were possible to obtain a single amendment to our Constitution. I would be

willing to depend on that alone for the reduction of the administration of our government; I mean an additional article taking from the Federal Government the power of borrowing ..."

17. In 1811 the charter of the First Bank of the United States was not renewed.

18. One year later the War of 1812 erupted. The British and the Americans were at war once again. The Americans declared war in 1812 for several reasons, including trade restrictions brought about by Britain's ongoing war with France.

19. In 1814 the British captured and burned Washington D.C., but American victories in September 1814 and January 1815 repulsed all three British invasions in New York, Baltimore and New Orleans.

20. The Treaty of Ghent officially ended the war. On December 24, 1814 the members of the British and American negotiating teams signed and affixed their individual seals to the document which, once ratified by their respective governments, ended the war of 1812.

The Battle of New Orleans was fought after it was signed. However, the treaty was not in effect until it was ratified by both sides in February 1815. This was one month after the battle in New Orleans. The treaty ignored the grievances that led to war. American complaints of Indian raids, impressments, and blockades had ended when Britain's war with France ended in 1814, and they were never mentioned in the treaty. The treaty largely restored relations between the two nations to "status quo ante bellum" (a Latin phrase meaning "the state existing before the war") with no loss of territory either way.

21. In 1816 yet another central bank was created. The Second Bank of the United States was established and it was given a 20-year charter. The Second Bank was chartered by many of the same congressional representatives who in 1811 had refused to renew the charter of the original Bank of the United States. The main reason that the Second Bank of the United States was chartered was that in the War of 1812 the U.S. experienced severe inflation, and had difficulty in financing military operations.

22. In 1828 Andrew Jackson (who had led the Battle of New Orleans during the war of 1812) became president. Jackson was determined to end the power of the central bankers over the United States

23. In 1832 Andrew Jackson's re-election slogan was "JACKSON and NO BANK!" His opponents took his slogan and changed it to "jackass and no bank". Jackson was a Democrat, and this was when the donkey became a political mascot for the party. An early renewal bill for the central bank was passed before the vote for Jackson's second election term. This bill was meant to pressure Jackson politically into signing the bill. Jackson vetoed the bill and made a speech concerning this event.

24. On July 10th 1832 President Jackson said this about the dangers of a central bank:

"It is not our own citizens only who are to receive the bounty of our government. More than eight millions of the stock of this bank are held by foreigners… is there no danger to our liberty and independence in a bank that in its nature has so little to bind it to our country? … Controlling our currency, receiving our public moneys, and holding thousands of our citizens in dependence… would be more formidable and dangerous than a military power of the enemy."

25. In January 1835 Jackson paid off the entire national debt. This is the only time in U.S. history that this has been accomplished.

26. President Jackson was strongly against the national bank. He vetoed the renewal of its charter and ensured its collapse in 1836.

27. On January 30, 1835 British-born Richard Lawrence attempted to shoot Andrew Jackson, but Jackson survived. There would be speculation that Lawrence was part of a conspiracy. While nobody denied Lawrence's involvement, many people (including Jackson) believed that he may have been supported by Jackson's political enemies. It should be noted that many people believe that Lawrence later admitted the bankers in Europe put him up to this, but that has never been proven.

28. The USA entered the period known as the "Free Banking Era", which lasted from 1837 to 1862. The only banks in the U.S. were those chartered by the states. The federal government neither chartered banks nor regulated the existing state banks. There were no federal laws regarding money. There was no federal income tax.

29. The Supreme Court ruled in Briscoe vs. Bank of Kentucky that state banks and the notes they issued were constitutional. States were the only government powers regulating money. At this point gold and silver were still considered money.

(List continued in Chapter Four)

Chapter Four - New Federal Money Laws

Let's continue our journey through America's real money history. Up until this time central banks had limited charters and there were no federal laws that regulated money, but all of that was about to change. As the Civil War broke out, states demanded to leave the Union. Something needed to be done to finance the Union Army. Let's continue with the next event.

30. Many people felt that The Civil War presented another opportunity for the bankers to get control of America. President Abraham Lincoln needed money for the war. He went with his Secretary of the Treasury Solomon P. Chase to get loans to finance the war. The banks in New York offered the Union loans that had an interest rate between 24 – 36%, but Lincoln declined.

31. An old friend of Lincoln's, Colonel Dick Taylor of Chicago, was put in charge of solving the problem of how to finance the Civil War. His solution was recorded as this:

"Just get Congress to pass a bill authorizing the printing of full legal tender treasury notes... and pay your soldiers with them and go ahead and win your war with them also."

32. Therefore, Lincoln pushed through the Legal Tender Act of 1862. Under that act, the U.S. government printed debt-free money known as "greenbacks" because of the green ink on the back of the notes. The U.S. printed $450 million in interest-free greenbacks from 1862 to 1864. Abraham Lincoln then founded the Secret Service, whose original job was to find and prosecute counterfeiters.

33. Three years later Abraham Lincoln was shot dead by John Wilkes Booth on April 14, 1865. The role of the Secret Service expanded as a result. In addition to tracking and ending counterfeit operations, they are now responsible for protecting the president.

34. After the Civil War, bankers purchased government bonds in exchange for bank notes. This was the system of currency in use at that time.

35. The National Banking Acts of 1863 and 1864 were two United States federal banking acts that established a system of national banks to supply the public banks, and created the United States National Banking System. They encouraged development of a national currency backed by the bank holdings of U.S. Treasury securities. These acts established the Office of the Comptroller of the Currency as part of the United States Department of the Treasury. It authorized the Comptroller to examine and regulate nationally chartered banks. The legacy of these federal banking acts is their impact on the national banking system as it stands today, and their support of a uniform national U.S. banking policy. National banks back then did many of the things that the Federal Reserve does today.

36. The United States was on the gold standard at that time. If a bank could not redeem its banknotes for real money like gold or silver, the bank had committed fraud, and it was subject to prosecution. If redemption demands exhausted their gold or silver reserves, these banks could rediscount the authentic bills in circulation to obtain gold or silver.

37. In 1866 Congress passed The Contraction Act, reducing the number of greenbacks in circulation. In 1866 there were 1.8 billion in circulation, but by 1876 there were only 600 million. At this point gold and silver could still be used as money.

38. James A. Garfield became president in 1881.Throughout Garfield's extended congressional service after the Civil War he fervently opposed the greenback. He gained a reputation as a skilled orator, and advocated a bi-metal monetary system.

39. Here is an actual quote from Garfield's inaugural address that shows his support of a bi-metal monetary system.

"The prosperity which now prevails is without parallel in our history. Fruitful seasons have done much to secure it, but they have not done all. The preservation of the public credit and the resumption of specie payments, so successfully attained by the Administration of my predecessors, have enabled our people to secure the blessings which the seasons brought.

By the experience of commercial nations in all ages it has been found that gold and silver afford the only safe foundation for a monetary system. Confusion has recently been created by variations in the relative Value of the two metals, but I confidently believe that arrangements can be made between the leading commercial nations which will secure the general use of both metals. Congress should provide that the compulsory coinage of silver now required by law may not disturb our monetary system by driving either metal out of circulation. If possible, such an adjustment should be made that the purchasing power of every coined dollar will be exactly equal to its debt-paying power in all the markets of the world.

The chief duty of the National Government in connection with the currency of the country is to coin money and declare its value. Grave doubts have been entertained whether Congress is authorized by the Constitution to make any form of paper money legal tender. The present issue of United States notes has been sustained by the necessities of war; but such paper should depend for its value and currency upon its convenience in use and its prompt redemption in coin at the will of the holder, and not upon its compulsory circulation. These notes are not money, but promises to pay money. If the holders demand it, the promise should be kept."

40. As you can see by his comments above, President Garfield considered the greenback unconstitutional if it was actually used as real money. To him the greenbacks were not legal tender. He believed that paper money should only operate as a claim check for metals. Garfield was shot by Charles J. Guiteau on July 2nd, 1881. He died from medical complications on September 19th, 1881.

41. The amount of greenbacks in circulation was greatly reduced due to The Contraction Act. This created a money supply shortage across the nation. As the population was increasing the money supply was shrinking.

42. In 1906 the U.S. stock market was doing well and setting records, but it began to decline toward the end of the year. In March of 1907 the U.S. stock market crashed. Numerous conspiracy theories allege that elite New York bankers were responsible.

43. The 1907 Bankers' Panic was a financial crisis that occurred in the United States when the New York Stock Exchange fell almost 50 percent from its peak the previous year. On March 12th of that year the Dow Jones Industrial Average was 86.53. On March 13th the market fell again and went to 83.12. On March 14th The Dow Jones Average crashed again and it was at

76.23. The next six months saw a steady decline in the stock market

A trust bank in those days was a commercial bank, organized to create the fiduciary of trusts and agencies. The "trust" part of the name refers to the ability of the institution's trust department to act as a trustee. This is someone who administers financial assets on behalf of another person. These trust companies were different from national banks and investment banks. These banks managed money on behalf of companies, estates, wills, and things of that nature. Many of these banks invested in the stock market and made loans to speculators. They took securities as collateral. When the stock market crashed it not only hurt the investors, it hurt the trust banks too.

On October 21st there was a run on The Knickerbocker Trust Co. The bank closed the next day after an auditor discovered that the bank's funds had been depleted. The bank's president shot himself. The Trust Company of America also suffered from a loss of public confidence. There was a run on it as well.

J.P. Morgan was called upon by President Teddy Roosevelt to help put an end to the panic, which he was able to do. Roosevelt gave him millions of dollars to distribute through these banks in order to end the panic. The panic of 1907 occurred during a lengthy economic contraction that lasted until June of 1908.

44. The panic of 1907 resulted in a congressional investigation that ended up concluding that a new central bank was necessary so that these kinds of panics would never happen again. It was determined that if they had had the ability to expand the money supply they could have avoided the catastrophe.

45. The Federal Reserve was set up about six years later. The legislation was written on Jekyll Island on Georgia's southern coast, and was pushed through by Senator Nelson Aldrich

46. The U.S. House of Representatives voted on the Federal Reserve Act on December 22nd, 1913. The Senate voted the next day on December 23, 1913. The Senate approved it by a vote of 43 yeas to 25 nays, with 27 abstaining.

47. It is widely believed that a significant portion of Congress was either sleeping at the time or was already at home with their families, celebrating the holidays.

48. The president that signed the bill into law that created the Federal Reserve was Woodrow Wilson. It is said by some conspiracy theorists that later on he wrote the following regarding his decision:

"A great industrial nation is controlled by its system of credit. Our system of credit is privately concentrated. The growth of the nation, therefore, and all our activities are in the hands of a few men who, even if their action be honest and intended for the public interest, are necessarily concentrated upon the great undertakings in which their own money is involved and who necessarily, by very reason of their own limitations, chill and check and destroy genuine economic freedom. This is the greatest question of all, and to this statesmen must address themselves with an earnest determination to serve the long future and the true liberties of men."

The truth is, he said something similar to this while on the campaign trail in 1912 but he was referencing the system that the Federal Reserve replaced, not the Federal Reserve itself! We will discuss this in detail later.

49. The new central bank needed to be funded just like our other central banking systems were funded - through various taxation systems. In 1913 the 16th Amendment was added to the Constitution. This made the income tax a permanent part of the U.S. tax system.

50. Between 1922 and 1930 the Federal Reserve increased the U.S. money supply by 62%, about 7% a year on average. This was a period of great prosperity known as "The Roaring 20s".

51. In addition to all of this, many people invested in the stock market, and most people made money from the market.

52. In October of 1929 the stock market began to crash. As a result the New York bankers started calling in margin loans on a massive scale. That created the initial crash that launched the Great Depression.

53. Instead of expanding the money supply in response to the crisis, the Federal Reserve decided to contract the money supply. This action only made things worse, leading to deflation and prolonging the Great Depression.

54. It has been reported that the U.S. money supply contracted by eight billion dollars between 1929 and 1933, an extraordinary amount of money in those days. Over one-third of all U.S. banks went bankrupt. Some of the New York bankers were able to buy up other banks, along with numerous other assets for pennies on the dollar. Some people gained wealth while many others became poor.

55. Every major currency left the gold standard after the Great Depression during the 1930s. This put an end to what is known as the classical gold era. Great Britain was the first to do so. Facing an onslaught of speculative attacks on the pound, and in turn depleting gold reserves, in September 1931 the Bank of England ceased exchanging pound notes for gold and the pound was floated on the foreign exchange. America was removed from the classic gold standard by FDR on June 5th 1933 after having been on it since 1879.

On April 5, 1933, FDR ordered all gold coins and gold certificates in denominations of more than $100 turned in for other money through executive order 6102. This order required all persons to deliver all gold coin, gold bullion, and gold certificates owned by them to the Federal Reserve by May 1 for the set price of $20.67 per ounce. By May 10 the government had taken in $300 million worth of gold coins and $470 million worth of gold certificates.

56. The United States Gold Reserve Act of January 30th 1934 required that all gold and gold certificates held by the Federal Reserve be surrendered and vested in the sole title of the United States Department of the Treasury.

The Gold Reserve Act outlawed most private possession of gold, forcing individuals to sell it to the Treasury. The U.S. Exchange Stabilization Fund or "ESF" was established at the Treasury Department by a provision in the Gold Reserve Act of January 30th 1934. (31 US Code U.S.C. § 5117) The Gold Reserve Act authorized the ESF to use such assets for exchange market stabilization to deal in government securities. They basically became a controlling arm for the Federal Reserve.

57. The classical gold era was brought to an end largely because of the Great Depression. People were hoarding gold, which brought the economy to a standstill. There were many problems with that system of exchange, so it was replaced by the Gold Reserve Act.

All gold and gold certificates held by the Federal Reserve had to be surrendered and vested in the sole title of the United States Department of the Treasury. Private possession of gold was outlawed, forcing individuals and corporations to sell it to the Treasury. It became illegal to conduct any transaction using gold. The Treasury stored the gold in the United States Bullion Depository at Fort Knox and three other locations.

The Banking Act of 1935 rewrote the laws regarding the Federal Reserve Act of 1913. The entire structure of the Federal Reserve Act was changed in this bill. Congress' constitutional power to "regulate the value of money" was a power that could not be delegated by executive order, and yet we see that these events taking place without congressional approval in the 1930s.

58. The Bretton Woods system eventually replaced the classical gold era and set up an international central banking system through the IMF, providing a fixed exchange rate system. In the process of building an international economic system as World War II was still raging, 730 delegates from all 44 Allied nations gathered at the Mount Washington Hotel in Bretton Woods, New Hampshire.

Under this new system, a country's government decides the worth of its currency in terms of either a fixed weight of gold, a fixed amount of another currency, or a collection of currencies also known as a basket of currencies. The central bank of a country remains committed at all times to buy and sell its currency at a fixed price, and provides the foreign currency needed to finance payment imbalances.

59. The Bretton Woods system was set up after World War II. The European Recovery

Program (or "ERP") was an American initiative to aid Western Europe, and to help them rebuild after World War II. (Don't confuse this plan with The European Economic Recovery Plan of 2008.) The ERP was also known as the Marshall Plan, named after Secretary of State George Marshall. It was in the process of implementing this plan that the Bretton Woods system emerged.

60. Due to the cost of the Vietnam War, the space race, and new entitlement spending aka the War on Poverty, America's spending was out of control in the late 1960s. We had more dollars in circulation than gold to back those dollars. Nations around the world were nervous because of the debt America began to accumulate. They wanted to cash their reserves in for our gold. Because of this, the decision was made to end dollar to gold conversion on August 15,1971 by Richard Nixon.

This ended the Bretton Woods system, and a fixed rate system for our currency was now traded for a floating rate system. Gold was no longer used to redeem U.S. paper in other countries. This event, known as the "Nixon Shock", was only supposed to be temporary but the Bretton Woods system was never reinstated. Many speculate that our currency became fiat at this time, and that every nation that used the U.S. dollar as a reserve became fiat as well. Gold was still used to back currencies, however.

61. Once we were removed from the Bretton Woods system, the petrodollar system was set up. By this time the U.S. dollar made its way into most central banks around the world. The United States entered into agreements with Saudi Arabia, and soon OPEC and other oil producing nations joined as well. We agreed to protect these nations with our military and we promised them wealth. The only thing we asked for in return is that these nations sell their oil for U.S. dollars only. This places value on our currency overseas as nearly every nation around the world now needs dollars to buy oil.

This agreement is officially called "The U.S.-Saudi Arabian Joint Commission on Economic Cooperation". It was negotiated by Henry Kissinger and was set up shortly after the oil embargo. Today most people refer to it simply as the petrodollar system.

62. The U.S. suffered through the 1973 oil crisis, starting in October of 1973 and lasting through March of 1974. While the main reason cited by the media for the crisis was a shortage of oil supply around the world, it was later discovered that it was due to an actual oil embargo. The Arab nations say that the embargo was in response to the U.S. decision to resupply the Israeli military during the Yom Kippur war.

63. Oil was now sold internationally using U.S. dollars, making it one of the world's main currencies at the time. The embargo drove the cost of oil up, and raised the demand for U.S. dollars around the world. The members of the Organization of Arab Petroleum Exporting Countries or "OAPEC" (made up from the Arab members of OPEC plus Egypt, Syria and Tunisia) enforced the embargo.

64. The energy crisis hit America hard, and drove the price of oil up even more through the rest of the 1970's. Inflation made a big impact during this time, and interest rates skyrocketed in an effort to get it under control. Jimmy Carter started the Department of Energy in 1977. All of this served to increase global demand for the dollar as supply and demand issues for oil arose. Jobs continued to be exported as other nations sought to import industry in order to obtain U.S. dollars so that they could buy oil.

65. On September 11, 2001 America was attacked when four airplanes were hijacked. Two of these planes flew into the World Trade Center, one plane flew into the Pentagon, and the last plane crashed in rural Pennsylvania. These events affected America's economy and the stock market fell as soon as it opened. The focus of the nation moved to wartime policies. America rebounded quickly.

66. America's economy crashed in a meltdown that occurred in 2008. This had global impact as national economies around the world suffered the same fate. A few years later China called for a new global currency to replace the dollar. The Federal Reserve began to buy toxic assets held by investors. They started their controversial QE program. Gold began to skyrocket in price shortly after the 2008 meltdown.

My Observations

Do most Americans know this history today? Of course not! In fact, it's a rare thing that an American can even adequately explain what a central bank is, much less explain what it does. It is critical that we educate as many Americans as possible about what is really going on in our financial institutions. Many conspiracy theories about our banking system are used to exploit people who don't know this history! These conspiracy theories are designed to scare people into buying things they would not normally purchase. The more we learn about the real history of the banking system the more we disarm the scam artists, and prevent them from selling people products they don't need.

While there are some wild conspiracy theories surrounding the earliest banks, America's monetary history, and the Rothschild dynasty, I can't help but make one observation. Those in a position of leadership who helped the bankers got support from those very bankers. Those in a position of leadership who opposed the bankers found themselves targeted and persecuted. This may go beyond coincidence, simply because of the frequency of events.

I have also observed that anyone who had anything to do with our money and forming its laws is featured on our paper currency. Let's explore this further,

1. George Washington signed the first central bank into law. He is on the one dollar bill.

2. Thomas Jefferson opposed the first central bank, according to our nation's history. He is on the two dollar bill.

3. Abraham Lincoln pushed through the Legal Tender Act, enabling the federal government to issue its own currency, the greenback. He is on the five dollar bill.

4. Alexander Hamilton supported the first central banking structure and it failed. He was also the chief supporter for its predecessor, The Bank of North America. He was also our nation's first treasurer. He is on the ten dollar bill.

5. Andrew Jackson paid off the national debt and ended the central bank's power to issue currency. He started the era known as the free banking era, allowing states to regulate money instead of the federal government. He is on the twenty dollar bill

6. Ulysses S. Grant was our 18th president. There was a panic in 1873 that led to a depression for five years. People wanted more

paper currency in circulation. The Contraction Act reduced the supply. The Inflation Bill was pushed through on April 14, 1874 to increase the nation's tight money supply. Many farmers and workers favored the bill, but Eastern bankers wanted a veto because of their reliance on bonds and foreign investors. On April 22, 1874 Grant unexpectedly vetoed the bill on the grounds that it would destroy the credit of the nation. He is on our 50 dollar bill.

7. Benjamin Franklin represented the U.S. before parliament in England several times. He gave an account of colonial script, the money used by the colonists. After these events England issued the Stamp Act. He is on our 100 dollar bill.

8. William McKinley was our 25th president. He secured the passage of the Gold Standard Act. He is on the 500 dollar bill. (No longer in circulation)

9. Grover Cleveland was the 22nd and 24th President of the United States. He was the only president to serve two non-consecutive terms. (1885–1889 and 1893–1897) In his second term the Panic of 1893 struck the nation. The panic was made worse by the acute shortage of gold that resulted from the free coinage of silver. Cleveland oversaw the repeal of the Sherman Silver Act. At the time, the repeal seemed a minor setback to silverites, but it marked the beginning of the end of silver as a basis for American money. Cleveland is on our 1,000 dollar bill. (No longer in circulation)

10. James Madison led an opposition against the First Bank of The United States (our first official central bank). He is on the 5,000 dollar bill. (No longer in circulation)

11. Salmon Portland Chase was an American politician and jurist who served as a U.S.

Senator. He served as Secretary of the Treasury in President Lincoln's cabinet from 1861 to 1864, during the time of the Civil War. There were two great changes in American financial policy, the establishment of a national banking system and the issuance of paper currency (the greenback). He is on our 10,000 dollar bill. (No longer in circulation)

12. Woodrow Wilson was the man who gave us the Internal Revenue Service via the 16th Amendment, signed the Federal Reserve Act into law, and created our last central bank! He is on our 100,000 dollar bill. (No longer in circulation)

It is interesting to note that the ink on the back of the $100,000 bill that the Federal Reserve used is RED! Irony thou art a cruel beast! If you want to see what any of these original notes looked like, a quick Google search will bring up images of all of them.

Rewriting History For The GCR Agenda

There is a good reason that we spent the first 4 chapters of this book studying monetary history. Most conspiracy theories involving money will rewrite history and distort historic events. They will highlight some events while ignoring others because it serves their agenda. So we spent some time learning the real history in order to debunk the conspiracy theories. Many fake quotes are attributed to our Founding Fathers. Let me give you a few from Benjamin Franklin. These quotes cannot be sourced from any of his writings or any other records.

- *"That is simple. In the colonies we issue our own money. It is called Colonial Script. We issue it in proper proportion to the demands of trade and industry to make the products pass easily from the producers to the consumers. In this manner, creating for ourselves our own paper money, we control its purchasing power, and we have no interest to pay to no one."*

- *"In one year, the conditions were so reversed that the era of prosperity ended, and a depression set in, to such an extent that the streets of the Colonies were filled with unemployed."*
- *"The colonies would gladly have borne the little tax on tea and other matters had it not been that England took away from the colonies their money, which created unemployment and dissatisfaction. The inability of the colonists to get power to issue their own money permanently out of the hands of George III and the international bankers was the prime reason for the Revolutionary War."*

These three quotes are considered to be true by many conspiracy theory websites, despite the fact that there is no proof or evidence that Benjamin Franklin ever said any of this. Here is another fake quote from James Garfield.

- *"Whoever controls the volume of money in our country is absolute master of all industry and commerce...and when you realize that the entire system is very easily controlled, one way or another, by a few powerful men at the top, you will not have to be told how periods of inflation and depression originate."*

There is no record of Garfield ever saying this, unless you happen to wander into a conspiracy website or you hear them in amateur documentaries. Unfortunately some of the quotes listed in this chapter have actually made their way into professionally made documentaries. Here is another fake quote by Nathan Rothschild.

- *"Either the application for the renewal of the charter is granted, or the United States will find itself involved in a most disastrous war."*

This quote was supposed to be the real reason behind the war of 1812. If you don't believe that, then you are considered uninformed. Nathan Rothschild also allegedly issued orders:

- *"Teach these impudent Americans a lesson. Bring them back to Colonial status."*

The problem with this quote is that England did not start the war with America. America was the first to declare war, and America attacked first. There were different reasons for the war of 1812, yet this quote has appeared all over the internet and has even made its way into several documentary films in an effort to further demonize the Rothschild dynasty. Each fake quote has an agenda and its own conspiracy theory.

It is said that Woodrow Wilson made these statements years after he signed the Federal Reserve into law.

- *"[Our] great industrial nation is controlled by its system of credit. Our system of credit is privately concentrated. The growth of the nation, therefore, and all our activities are in the hands of a few men who, even if their action be honest and intended for the public interest, are necessarily concentrated upon the great undertakings in which their own money is involved and who necessarily, by very reason of their own limitations, chill and check and destroy genuine economic freedom."*
- *"We have come to be one of the worst ruled, one of the most completely controlled and*

dominated, governments in the civilized world-- no longer a government by free opinion, no longer a government by conviction and the vote of the majority, but a government by the opinion and the duress of small groups of dominant men."

The truth is the first quote was rewritten. In addition to this it was taken out of context. It appeared in a speech in 1912 one year before the Federal Reserve came into existence. Woodrow Wilson was addressing the system he wanted to change, not the one he put in place! Here is the actual quote.

- *"A great industrial nation is controlled by its system of credit. Our system of credit is privately concentrated. The growth of the nation, therefore, and all our activities are in the hands of a few men who, even if their action be honest and intended for the public interest, are necessarily concentrated upon the great undertakings in which their own money is involved and who necessarily, by very reason of their own limitations, chill and check and destroy genuine economic freedom."*

The second quote was also taken out of context. This is actually from a 1912 campaign speech, and was also said before the Federal Reserve was formed and signed into law! The agenda here is to rewrite the quote just a little in order to demonize the Federal Reserve. Here is the real quote.

- *"We have restricted credit, we have restricted opportunity, we have controlled development, and we have come to be one of the worst ruled, one of the most completely controlled and dominated, governments in the civilized world-- no longer a government by free opinion, no longer a government by conviction and the vote of the majority, but a government by the opinion and the duress of small groups of dominant men."*

Conspiracy theorists also claim that Alexander Hamilton was a Rothschild agent who worked on behalf of the family. They even claim that he married into their family. The truth is Hamilton's father-in-law Philip Schuyler was a general during the Revolutionary War, and his mother-in-law Catherine conducted a scorched earth policy to deprive the British of food. He never married into the Rothschild family.

The main problem with this theory is that the house of Rothschild was not set up until 1776, the same year America declared her independence. The Rothschilds didn't become major players in the banking system until the 1800s. Alexander Hamilton argued on behalf of the first central bank long before this. It was signed into law by George Washington in 1791. Although it was possible for the Rothschild family to have a degree of controlling interest in the first central bank, Hamilton never married into the family and had no influence on their behalf. The timeline just doesn't match up.

Most Americans don't know this history, and therefore don't recognize that it is being misrepresented in order to portray the current system as a sinister plot set up by a cabal that is taking over the world. It is widely preached that the Federal Reserve is the system that the Cabal or Illuminati uses to control the world economy, and it will soon come crashing down all around us. The only thing you can do to protect yourself is to buy emergency food supplies, prepper supplies, gold, and silver. They will show you how to do this through their scummy newsletters for a modest subscription fee. Exotic foreign currencies like the Iraqi dinar and the Vietnamese dong are also peddled by the GCR crowd as means of protection against a falling dollar.

By now you should see the agenda pretty clearly! These people can be divided into two groups. First you have the merchants who are behind the hype. Then you have the converts who believe the hype. These people are trapped in this conspiratorial environment that is very similar to a cult. I just showed you seven fake quotes that are constantly used by the GCR people, but there are many more.

As Abraham Lincoln once said "Don't believe everything you read on the internet!"

Chapter Five - The Global Economy Emerges

Perhaps the most amazing thing to see in modern times is the emergence of a one-world government. George H. W. Bush called it "A New World Order". Along with this new global government we see a new global economy taking shape. It is important to gain an understanding of this system and where it came from in order to grasp what the Global Currency Reset crowd believes.

To understand how we got this global economy we need to go back to the Frankfurt am Main (modern day Frankfurt) in Germany in the year 1744, where and when Mayer Amschel Bauer was born. Bauer became a moneylender and changed his last name to Rothschild, which means "red shield". He and his five sons marked the beginning of the Rothschild dynasty. Mayer set his sons up in key locations throughout Europe. Nathan went to London, Salomon went to Vienna, Calamann went to Naples, Jakob went to Paris, and Anselm stayed in Frankfurt. Together they created central banking institutions. They loaned money to governments and started controlling currencies, and their descendants maintain and control central banks around the world to this day.

During our industrial age of the 19th and early 20th centuries there arose what are often referred to as the "titans of industry". They included the world's first billionaires. Their business ventures shaped and molded us through a period of time known as The Gilded Age, a term coined by Mark Twain. The Rothschild family, J.P. Morgan, John D

Rockefeller, Andrew Carnegie, Cornelius Vanderbilt, and Henry Ford were all part of an elite class of titans that helped to modernize America.

John Rockefeller owned Standard Oil. He was ruthless to the competition and drove a lot of them out of business, which culminated in a 1911 antitrust lawsuit from the U.S. government. When Standard Oil was broken up by the government he made a vast sum of money, making him the wealthiest man in America at the time. He and his son became involved in banking and other business ventures, and created a non-profit organization called The Rockefeller Foundation.

Through the foundation his family provided funding for the Council on Foreign Relations (or "CFR") and The Trilateral Commission. These are globalist organizations with the goal of bringing about a global economy and government. Conspiracy theorists refer to this as a New World Order (or "NWO"). The CFR was established in 1921, and is now considered the nation's most influential foreign policy think tank. They also control much of the mainstream media.

It is widely preached by conspiracy theorists that the Federal Reserve is a private bank rather than a government bank. They also claim that the Rockefeller, Rothschild, Aldrich, and Morgan families were all involved in the creation of the Federal Reserve Act in 1913. These families and aristocrats supposedly worked behind the scenes, and were also involved in the creation of the global empire and the global economy. These are said to be actions of a cabal. Some see it as the Illuminati working behind the scenes. Various versions of these conspiracy theories can be found all over the internet, but there's a lot of fiction mixed with actual events in order to make things seem more plausible. Due to the fact that most people don't know the economic details, they fall prey to the distortions. The Federal Reserve is at the center of almost every economic conspiracy theory, so let's explore some of the relevant facts.

An organization known as the League of Nations was formed out of the Paris Peace Conference that took place six years after the formation of the Federal Reserve. The same Rockefeller organization that funded the CFR also helped in funding the League of Nations and many other ventures. From this you can see the beginnings of a one-world government, but it has no teeth at this point.

Andrew Carnegie was a Scottish American industrialist who led the enormous expansion of the American steel industry in the late 19th century. When J.P. Morgan purchased his steel factory it made Carnegie the richest man in the world. Toward the end of his life he also started a foundation that often collaborated with The Rockefeller Foundation. These foundations donated large sums of money to universities around the world and contributed to global causes.

After World War II this one-world government began to take shape. The League of Nations was considered a failure because they failed to stop Hitler in his conquest for Europe. In 1945 The United Nations replaced The League of Nations. The Rockefeller family donated all of the land needed to build the new facility in New York City that has housed the UN up until the time of this writing.

The UN wasted no time seizing world power. After WWII Europe was in need of rebuilding, and the Marshall Plan became the blueprint for that project. It was a large-scale American program to aid Europe. This is how the plan worked.

The United States gave monetary support to help rebuild European economies after World War II. This was done in order to combat the spread of Soviet communism. The plan was in operation for four years beginning in April of 1948. The goals of the United States were to rebuild a war-devastated region, modernize industry, remove trade barriers, and make Europe prosperous again.

Around this same period a few more global organizations became established, and many were placed under the umbrella of the United Nations.

International Monetary Fund (IMF)

The International Monetary Fund was born out of a conference called the United Nations Monetary and Financial Conference in July of 1944 held in Bretton Woods, New Hampshire by the soon-to-be United Nations. The IMF was formally organized on December 27, 1945 when the first 29 countries signed its articles of agreement. The statutory purposes of the IMF today are the same as when they were first formulated – to promote global monetary cooperation, financial stability, trade, employment, economic growth, and prosperity.

International Bank for Reconstruction and Development (IBRD)

The IBRD was established mainly as a vehicle for reconstruction of Europe and Japan after World War II, with an additional mandate to foster economic growth in developing countries in Africa, Asia, and Latin America. It began operations on June 25, 1946 and approved its first loan on May 9, 1947. The IBRD later became part of The World Bank.

Bretton Woods System

When the European nations were being rebuilt, they had to sign on to the Bretton Woods System in order to get international assistance. These nations surrendered a lot of their sovereignty to the new international laws that were being made at that time. They also had to accept a new monetary system. The Bretton Woods system of monetary management established the international laws for commercial and financial relations among the world's major industrial countries in the mid-20th century. The Bretton Woods system was the first example of a negotiated monetary structure intended to govern monetary relations among independent nations.

While planning to build a new international economic system as World War II was still raging, some 730 delegates from all of the 44 allied nations gathered at the Mount Washington Hotel in Bretton Woods, New Hampshire. There they deliberated and signed the Bretton Woods Agreements during the first three weeks of July 1944. This same conference gave us the IMF and IBRD.

The new system worked like this. After World War II America had about 80 percent of the world's gold supply because the American government confiscated as much gold as they could after 1933. America also acquired gold from other nations once FDR abandoned the gold standard. The U.S. issued currency to other nations based on that gold. Other nations held U.S. currency in their reserves and based their currency's value off of our dollar. Nations throughout the world now held the dollar in their reserves to back their currency. The U.S. dollar was internationally backed by gold.

It is important to note that America was still removed from the classic gold standard. Bretton Woods was more of a quasi-international gold system. When nations like Japan were rebuilt under the Marshall Plan they also signed on to the Bretton Woods system. Even though money was still redeemable in silver and gold before August 15, 1971, by the time Bretton Woods was implemented gold was normally used as an asset. The limitation on gold ownership no longer existed by the time Bretton Woods was in place. Anyone could own any amount of gold they wanted, but it was seldom used in local commerce or to settle debts, and it rarely functioned as money in America's economy. Gold was removed entirely when Richard Nixon announced that the U.S. would abandon Bretton Woods.

General Agreement on Tariffs and Trade (GATT)

The General Agreement on Tariffs and Trade is typically abbreviated as GATT. It was negotiated during the UN Conference on Trade and Employment. GATT was the result of the failure of negotiating governments to create the International Trade Organization or ITO. It was signed into international law in 1947 and lasted until 1995 when it was replaced by the World Trade Organization. The original GATT text of 1947 is still in effect under the WTO framework, and it is subject to the modifications of GATT 1994.

Most of these organizations fall under the United Nations. They came about in the mid to late 1940s as the international community began to take shape. Because of these global organizations, nations are now subject to international law and UN mandates.

The Petrodollar

In the 1960s nations around the world watched our debt skyrocket during the Johnson and Nixon administrations. Entitlement spending, the War on Poverty, the Vietnam War, the Space Race, and the Cold War were all draining America's pockets. Since foreign nations had their currency backed by U.S. dollars, and since our dollars were backed internationally by gold, these nations wanted to trade the American dollars they held for the gold America had in its possession, and America's debt was the primary motivation. This would have completely drained America's gold supply as nations sought to back their currencies with gold.

For that reason on August 15, 1971 President Nixon ended the direct international convertibility of the U.S. dollar to gold, thus ending the Bretton Woods System. This is also known as the Nixon Shock. In doing so, Nixon ensured that all U.S. currencies held by other nations could not be redeemed for gold. After the Nixon Shock those currencies were now backed by our fiat paper dollar. (Fiat means money without intrinsic value. It is faith-based, and it only has value because of government law or decree.)

Federal law states that the United States dollar still needs to be backed by assets. Even though the dollar now technically falls into the definition of a fiat currency, most fiat currencies are not backed by assets. The gold that was around in 1971 is still in the possession of the United States, and it backs a percentage of the dollar supply as of this writing. (The rest of the money supply is backed by treasury bills, notes, bonds and other assets.) The main difference is you could no longer trade the dollar for the assets that backed it. This is one reason the dollar is still a fiat currency today by definition.

This became a problem on a global level. The sudden jump in the price of gold after the abrupt end of the Bretton Woods System was more than likely a result of the massive prior debasement of the U.S. dollar due to excessive inflation of the money supply via the central bank. The debasement happened through monetizing debt, and was coordinated through fractional reserve banking under the Bretton Woods partial gold standard system. This was done by the Federal Reserve System prior to the end of Bretton Woods.

Something had to be done to restore our currency value once again, and the petrodollar was born in the latter part of 1973. Henry Kissinger was instrumental in setting up this agreement. It works like this.

The Saudi nation entered into an agreement with the United States. Their part was simple. All they have to do is sell their oil for U.S. dollars only. Don't use any other currency. In return, the

United States promised Saudi Arabia military protection. This was important because the Saudi government did not have a strong military at the time. The United States also promised Saudi Arabia that they would become wealthy. Soon after the Saudi agreement was reached other Arab nations signed on to the same deal. That is why the United States had to go to war with Iraq on behalf of Kuwait in 1991. They had to honor the petrodollar arrangement.

This petrodollar created a strong global demand for the U.S. dollar. If you are a nation that does not have oil as a resource, you have to find a way to buy oil for your country. To make matters worse, you can only use U.S. dollars to get that oil. If you are a nation like Japan you only have two choices; exchange yen for dollars and buy oil, or sell the Americans a Toyota, Datsun, Honda, or Nintendo and use the tax revenues from those exports to buy oil.

Because of this new petrodollar system, manufacturing jobs in the 1970s began to be exported to foreign countries around the world where these goods could be made cheaper. This was done so that these countries could generate the U.S. dollars needed to buy oil. In the 1980s America began to export its manufacturing base on a larger scale, and that practice accelerated throughout the 1980s and into the 1990s. Nations also started trading with each other using more U.S. dollars. Global demand for the dollar actually rose after Bretton Woods ended. The global demand did not diminish as many people had anticipated at that time. It seemed as though this petrodollar system was pure genius!

The petrodollar has been the new system since Bretton Woods. It is the main cause of the globalization of our economy. This petrodollar system gives the U.S. fiat dollar value around the world. This is because the petrodollar creates a demand for the U.S. currency abroad. If America wants to import more oil, all it has to do is print more dollars.

Some may argue that our dollar is not a total fiat currency as gold merchants claim. Today our dollar gets a lot of strength from oil. America has successfully convinced the oil-producing nations to back our currency. In addition to this, these nations have agreed to take some of the profits made from selling oil and put those profits back into the U.S. by investing in U.S. bonds. This is brilliant! America gets foreign nations to back their currency with their oil, and then they get these nations to buy our debt!

This new system is not perfect, however. The petrodollar system has created many problems. Nations fight to keep their currency values low because this acts as a tariff on imported goods. That's why the Chinese yuan has been kept artificially low. Nations with low currency values benefit because this practice serves to accelerate their manufacturing base. The higher your currency value, the less you export and the more your economy imports.

An artificially low value acts as a tariff on imported goods. If nations want to keep a low value on their currency all they need to do is print a lot of currency. The more currency they have the lower the value. This is why nations print their currency into oblivion. The Vietnamese have printed over 5 quadrillion dong. That is a lot of currency!

Another problem with the petrodollar system is that America lost a lot of its manufacturing base to overseas markets. Jobs started to leave the United States in the 1970s. Countries needed these jobs to get U.S. dollars, and they needed those dollars to buy oil. The job losses accelerated in the first decade of the new millennium as China became a member of the World Trade Organization (or "WTO").

The Global Currency Reset merchants need to explain how the dollar could suddenly collapse while the petrodollar system is in place! This is something they can't do! As long as oil is sold in dollars around the world there will be global demand for the dollar. Every oil-producing nation will need to abandon the sale of oil in dollars overnight in order for the dollar to completely crash as these people claim. Given the amount of dollars and treasury bills these Arab nations hold, it is highly unlikely that they will all of a sudden abandon the dollar overnight and forsake their holdings because that would greatly reduce their wealth!

The dollar is still a fiat currency by every sense of the definition. The only difference between the dollar and other fiat currencies is that the dollar is backed with real assets even though those assets are not redeemable. The petrodollar actually makes the case that if the dollar is abandoned and traded out, it will be on a gradual basis so these nations can preserve their wealth!

The Trilateral Commission

The Trilateral Commission is a non-governmental, non-partisan discussion group founded by David Rockefeller in July 1973 to foster closer cooperation among the United States, Europe and Japan, thus completing this new global structure.

When George H. W. Bush came to Kuwait's defense in 1991 he announced a "New World Order" coming into view.

"Until now, the world we've known has been a world divided—a world of barbed wire and concrete block, conflict and cold war. Now, we can see a new world coming into view. A world in which there is the very real prospect of a new world order. In the words of Winston Churchill, a "world order" in which "the principles of justice and fair play ... protect the weak against the strong ..." A world where the United Nations, freed from cold war stalemate, is poised to fulfill the historic vision of its founders. A world in which freedom and respect for human rights find a home among all nations." – George H Bush

So now we have international laws, international trade, an international economy, and an international government headquartered at the United Nations in New York City.

In all of this the dollar is king. The dollar brought us to this point. One of the theories behind the Global Currency Reset is that a new international currency or a basket of currencies will replace the dollar. There are people who claim that when this happens, America's economy will collapse. Nations will stop selling oil in dollars, and use this new international currency or basket of currencies instead. This will cause all currencies around the globe to reset in value. The rationale is that the dollar is highly overprinted, and will collapse as all fiat currencies do when they are overprinted.

Is there any truth to this Global Currency Reset? Let's investigate this idea a bit further. Now that we have the history portion finished, the next thing we need to do is to learn some simple money mechanics. I promise to make this as painless as possible.

Chapter Six - Simple Money Mechanics

I just want to take some time to explain some simple money mechanics. It is important to know these principles in order to gain a better understanding of the GCR. This is just an effort to make sure that everyone is on the same page. If you know these basic principles, then you will be better equipped to understand everything you need to know about the theoretical GCR event.

Inflation

Inflation happens when the value and purchasing power of a currency decreases. Deflation has the opposite effect of inflation. With deflation, the value and purchasing power of currency increases. Three basic things can cause inflation. A counter balance of these three things can also cause deflation.

The first variable that can cause inflation is supply and demand. If there is a lot of demand for a particular product but little supply, the price should go up. If there is a big supply but little demand, the price will probably go down.

A good example of this can be found in oil. The oil embargo during the early 70's caused supply to go down. America entered what the main stream media called the energy crisis. It was believed that there was a major shortage of oil around the world. The price of oil went up and this led to the price of gas shooting up as well. This in turn causes everything else to go up. There was no major increase in the money supply, but the dollar lost purchasing power due to the supply and demand for oil. Interest rates were raised to combat the inflation. This action typically reduces the money supply and causes deflation as less debt is monetized. This had little effect in the first few years as this sudden increase of inflation was not caused by the money supply.

Many years later Saudi Arabia flooded the global market with oil in order to drive the American companies that were exploring fracking out of business. The overabundance of oil in the market drove prices down. This action caused gas prices to go down significantly.

The second thing that can cause inflation is cost. When things cost more to make, or costs associated with the sale of any given product go up, it squeezes the profit margin. In most cases these costs get passed on to consumers as the price to produce those goods increases.

Once again, A good example of this is the price of gas. When the cost of gas increases, it cost more to bring goods to market. As a result, the higher cost of fuel is passed on to consumers. That is why grocery prices normally go up with the rising cost of fuel. When costs go down prices can be reduced, which in turn causes greater sales and higher profit margins. This happened during the 2008 meltdown. The price of oil went over $148 dollars a barrel and food skyrocketed in price.

Another example can be found in the minimum wage. Higher labor costs will probably bring higher service and commodity prices. Recently California raised their minimum wage to 15 dollars an hour. This is well above the federal minimum wage. As a result, business responded by raising prices on goods and services and cutting jobs.

The third thing that causes inflation is the money supply. When the supply of money dramatically increases and more money becomes available to the public, the cost of everything goes up as people have more money to spend. This is the danger of printing too much currency.

The Federal Reserve became operational during the second decade of the 1900s, during World War I. Their first major task was to support the U.S. Treasury's wartime financing needs. Most of the credit they created was during the years 1916–1920. This credit was meant to support Liberty Loans the government floated to help finance the war and its aftermath. Their subsequent contraction of credit in 1920 contributed significantly to the recession and the deflation that occurred in 1921–1922.

Average Inflation Rates Per Year
1914-1.0 percent
1915-1.0 percent
1916-7.9 percent
1917-17.4 percent
1918-18 percent (In November of 1918 the inflation rate for that month alone was 20.7%)
1919-14.6 percent
1920-15.6 percent
1921- negative 10.5 percent

The economy quickly recovered after 1922, and America headed into the Roaring '20s. By 1929 the money supply was expanded by 62 percent.

Meanwhile, margin loans created access to the stock market. Anyone could now invest in the market due to these loans. This extra debt also aided in the expansion of the money supply during the '20s, but much of it did not enter into general circulation. This kept inflation from rising dramatically, but ultimately this very loan process sparked the Great Depression. The Feds began to contract the money supply after 1929. At the same time the federal government began to confiscate America's privately held gold, removing even more resources from the public. All these circumstances led to deflation, and served to prolong the Great Depression for over a decade.

Since the Federal Reserve took over in 1913, our money supply has been expanding at an unprecedented rate. The cumulative rate of inflation since 1913 has been 2302.5%. Today our money supply has been so debased and expanded that the value of 1 dollar in 1913 is equivalent to $24.39 in 2016. Twenty dollars in 1913 is equivalent in value to $487.73 in 2016.

It is amazing to see how much the money supply has expanded in America since 1913. It's important to note that there has also been a great increase in the population. If the money supply is not expanded to coincide with population growth it can cause deflation and poverty, as there is not enough currency to keep the economy moving. We saw this in the later part of the 19th century. If it is expanded too much however, it will cause inflation.

The GCR crowd would have everyone believe that inflation is only caused by the amount of money that is in circulation. As we have just seen, that is not true. These people coined the term "inflating the money supply" as if to imply this point. Then they will point to times in American history when inflation or deflation happened by some other means. Then they will try to make the point that inflating the money supply brings about some of the major catastrophes we witness like the oil embargo or the 2008 meltdown. That is simply not the case and the scenarios they set up are really deceitful. I coined a term to describe some of this flawed analysis. I call it "Junk Economics".

Hyperinflation

Hyperinflation occurs when a country experiences accelerating rates of inflation. With hyperinflation the local currency will always rapidly lose real value, and in most cases it is due to a rapidly growing money supply. When hyperinflation sets in we see a rapid and continuing increase in the price level of goods and services within an economy as the official national currency quickly loses value.

In most cases the cure for hyperinflation is a drastic reduction of the money supply. This happens through a process called "redenomination". The process is sometimes described as "removing the zeros", and involves issuing a new series of currency to replace the old series of currency. Through this process, the money supply becomes drastically reduced. Usually there is a trade-in period where the old series of currency is exchanged for the new series. After the trade-in period expires, the old series of currency becomes demonetized and invalid.

A redenomination has become a common way to fight hyperinflation and restore value to currency. There have been over 70 redenominations around the world between 1970 and 2005.

Money Creation and the Federal Reserve

When our government creates treasury bills and bonds they are sold to bankers and private parties for U.S. dollars. The Federal Reserve creates money through a monetary policy known as "open market operations". The Fed buys financial assets like treasury bills, government bonds, or foreign currencies from banks and private parties. The central bank creates the money on the spot for these assets. While some will claim that nothing backs the money the Federal Reserve creates, the money the Feds create is solely based on the value of the asset they purchase. This is how the base money supply is created. Purchases of these assets result in new currency entering market circulation and the public banking system.

When the Federal Reserve decides to sell these assets, the money supply is reduced as the Feds take back the money they created. This is one way they control the base money supply - through expansion and contraction.

Only a small percentage of America's currency supply is physical currency. It is printed by The United States Treasury Department and distributed through the Federal Reserve. It's done this way because our constitution requires this structure. The amount of our physical currency is called M0. The amount of our physical currency outside of the private banking structure is called M1

The amount of most electronic currency and physical currency is called M2. This is also known as our broad money supply. As I stated earlier, around two-thirds of our currency is

outside the borders of the United States where it is used in several ways, including:
- by other nations to conduct global commerce
- by citizens of other countries to conduct business
- as a reserve currency in central banks around the world
- as a medium of exchange in oil sales

Quantitative Easing involves the creation of new base money by the Federal Reserve through the purchasing of assets that the central bank usually does not buy. Normally the Feds will conduct open market operations by buying short-term government bonds or foreign currency. However, after the 2008 meltdown the Federal Reserve started buying other types of financial assets as well. These assets are extended to include long-term government bonds, stocks, commercial loans, company bonds, and asset-backed securities. The purpose of QE is to stimulate the economy by increasing liquidity and promoting bank lending, even when interest rates cannot go any lower.

It is important to know that new money put into circulation pulls value from the money that is already in circulation, and waters it down as a result. This is why adding money to the currency supply can cause inflation. This also means that taking money away from the currency supply could cause deflation. This is one of the main reason the Federal Reserve monitors currency supplies closely. Any expansion needs to coincide with a growing economy and population growth.

Fractional Reserve Banking

Fractional Reserve Banking is the process of expanding the money supply by monetizing debt through the public banking system. It is in operation whenever a bank accepts deposits and makes loans. This process holds reserves that are equivalent to a fraction of its deposit liabilities.

Fractional reserve banking (or "FRB") allows banks to act as financial intermediaries between borrowers and savers. This process provides longer-term loans to borrowers while at the same time providing immediate liquidity to depositors. Fractional reserve banking allows the money supply to grow beyond the amount of the base money originally created by the central bank. It works something like this.

Let's say a large business deposits $1,000,000 dollars into a bank account. That new deposit now becomes part of the bank's reserves. In fact, all deposits become bank reserves. According to a Federal Reserve publication known as Modern Money Mechanics, a bank must maintain required reserves equal to a prescribed percentage of its deposits. Typically the reserve requirements are ten percent.

This means that from our example, the bank has to keep $100,000 dollars from the million dollar deposit. The other $900,000 is considered an excessive reserve. It can and will be used for loans. You might think that the $900,000 is loaned from the original one million amount we started with. However, when this money is loaned it does not actually come out of the original million. When this $900,000 is loaned, it is newly created money on top of the already existing 1 million dollars for a total of 1.9 million dollars. This is how money is expanded through FRB. Debt is monetized and used to create new money!

"Of course, they do not really pay out loans from the money they receive as deposits. If they did this, no additional money would be created. What they do when they make loans is to accept promissory notes in exchange for credits to the borrowers' transaction accounts." -Modern Money Mechanics

Let's assume someone goes into the bank and borrows the $900,000 dollars from that original million dollar deposit. Chances are they take that money and deposit it in their own checking account and the process starts all over. The bank of the borrower now has $810,000 as an excessive reserve. They loan that money but they keep $90,000 as a reserve requirement. And on it goes! Through this process, the original one million dollars is typically expanded. This is how debt is monetized.

Before the Federal Reserve, paper money was a receipt that represented gold that someone had on deposit. After the Federal Reserve took over our money, the system slowly migrated to a system of debt where every expanded dollar represents an asset or an instrument of debt.

Money Stock

The money supply or money stock is the total amount of monetary assets available in an economy at any specific time. The different types of money stocks start with the capital letter M followed by a Number or a letter.

Not all of the classifications are widely used, and each country may use different definitions for the classification. Because of this, each classification may mean something different depending on the country. For example, In the United Kingdom M0 includes bank reserves, so M0 is also referred as the monetary base. This is how all the classifications break down.

M0 = The total of all physical currency including coinage. M0 = Federal Reserve Notes + US Notes + Coins. It does not matter whether the currency is inside or outside of the private banking system.

MB = The total of all physical currency plus Federal Reserve Deposits. These Fed deposits are special deposits that only banks can use at the Federal Reserve. MB = Coins + US Notes + Federal Reserve Notes + Federal Reserve Deposits

M1 = The total amount of M0 (cash/coin) outside of the private banking system plus the amount of demand deposits, travelers checks and other checkable deposits

M2 = M1 + most savings accounts, money market accounts, retail money market mutual funds, and small denomination time deposits (certificates of deposit of under $100,000).

MZM = Money Zero Maturity. This M is one of the most popular aggregates in use by the Federal Reserve today because it has historically been the most accurate predictor of inflation. It is made up of M2 − time deposits + money market funds

M3 = M2 + all other CDs (institutional money market mutual fund balances, large time deposits). It also includes deposits of euro-dollars and repurchase agreements.

M4- = M3 + Commercial Paper
M4 = M3 + Commercial Paper + T-Bills
L = M4 + Bankers' Acceptance

The Federal Reserve always published data on the M1, M2, and M3 supplies, but on November 10, 2005 the Federal Reserve announced that it will no longer report M3 data. Since March 2006 it stopped all publication of M3 data, and hasn't reported on the M3 supply since.

Expansion and Contraction of the Money Supply

Contractionary monetary policies and expansionary monetary policies involve changing the levels of the money supply. There are a few ways to do this, but before I explain the methods involved let's discuss why money is expanded and contracted.

An increase in the supply of money normally lowers interest rates. This in turn generates more investment, which creates more jobs and puts more money in consumers' pockets. In most cases, this will stimulate spending.

Businesses around the world respond by ordering more raw materials and increasing production. This increased business activity will always raise the demand for labor. The opposite usually occurs if the money supply falls too far.

The tradeoff for too much expansion is a higher inflation rate, which decreases the currency's value. Central bank policies attempt to balance inflation with economic growth. This is why the Federal Reserve will contract or expand the money supply.

The Federal Reserve may increase the interest rate at which it lends money. This action will also increase the rates at which banks lend money. When rates are higher it becomes more expensive for individuals to obtain loans. This will reduce consumer spending, along with the amount of debt. This is one way the money supply is contracted.

Banks are required to keep a reserve from cash deposits to meet withdrawal demands. In the past, this reserve requirement has been 10 percent. If the reserve requirements are increased the commercial bank has less money to lend out. As a result, there will be a lower money supply over time.

Notice that these two contraction measures involve the loan process. This is because all debt becomes monetized through the loan process, and it turns into money. As we stated earlier this happens through the process of fractional reserve banking. This also means that when debt is fully paid and removed from the books money is taken out of circulation.

After the 2008 meltdown, trillions of dollars vanished. This was due not only to wrongly perceived values in the housing market, but also to the abnormal amount of bankruptcies. Bankruptcy filings in 2008 rose 32% as compared to 2007. This was in part because credit was very limited, and in part because of the new unemployment rates. As debt was removed from the books through bankruptcy, money also vanished from circulation.

Central banks can also contract from the money supply by borrowing money from institutions or individuals by selling bonds. When the Federal Reserve increases the interest rate paid on these bonds, investors will be encouraged to buy them. As bond sales increase, more money is taken out of circulation. This also results in money flowing out of the stock market.

Central banks can also reduce the amount of money they lend out, or call in existing debts to reduce the money supply.

The Federal Reserve says that at any given time between one-half and two-thirds of the U.S. money supply (M0) is beyond our borders. Because the money overseas is not in circulation in America, it has no direct impact on inflation in the United States. This is not even counting the two-thirds of electronic currency which is also overseas.

Even though there's a lot of currency in print, only the currency in America has a direct impact on inflation or deflation in America. There is a lot of U.S. currency overseas that remains in central banks. This currency functions as a reserve to back other currencies. The currency overseas that is located in central bank reserves does not have a direct impact on inflation abroad because it is not in public circulation. Since 2008, there has actually been a dollar shortage in some countries. At the time of this writing, the global demand for dollars remains strong.

Revaluation and Devaluation

A free-floating currency is a unit of currency that is market driven. The market demand determines its value. An example of this can be found in the U.S. dollar, the euro, or the Japanese yen. Most major currencies are floating currencies.

A pegged currency, also known as a dirty float or a managed float, is a currency that is tied to a floating currency to get its value. These currencies usually have the floating currency that they are pegged to in their currency reserves. These reserves are kept in the pegged currency's central bank. The amount of the currency and other assets held in a country's central bank's reserves will determine the value of that country's currency in circulation. The ratio of value for a managed floating currency will typically match the amount of a country's currency verses the value of assets in the reserves.

A devaluation in a pegged currency means the pegged currency's value went down. A revaluation means the value of the pegged currency has gone up. The central banks of the pegged currency's country are the only ones that determine when to revalue or devalue. Typically revaluations and devaluations are small. They can be anywhere from 1 to 5 percent, although there have been some as high as 22 to 27 percent. They may take place all at once, or they might happen over a period of years. In all of history there has never been a revaluation of a currency above 50 percent. Usually a revaluation is done in an effort to lower inflation rates and stabilize the currency. Devaluation is usually done if the economy slows down and deflation sets in, or when the country wants to make their currency less valuable in an effort to attract buyers for their exports.

Keynesian Economics

Now we need to explain Keynesian Economics. This will give you a clearer understanding of the government's philosophy regarding economic policies. John Maynard Keynes developed his economic theory during the 1930s in an attempt to understand the Great Depression. He was a British economist, and his theory was not the popular school of thought at the time.

The central theme of this theory is that government intervention can stabilize the economy. Mr. Keynes started a revolution in economic thinking that overturned the prevailing belief that the free markets would automatically provide full employment for everyone and anyone who wanted a job. There are three main principles in the Keynesian description of how the economy works:

1. Aggregate demand (the total demand for final goods and services in an economy at a given time) is influenced by many economic decisions, both public and private.

2. Changes in aggregate demand, whether anticipated or unanticipated, have their greatest short-run effect on real output and employment, not on prices.

3. Prices, and especially wages, respond slowly to changes in supply and demand.

Keynes believed that inadequate overall demand could lead to prolonged periods of high unemployment. An economy's output of goods and services are the sum total of four components: consumption, investment, government purchases, and net exports. Therefore, any increase in demand has to come from one of these four components.

When people save money and don't spend enough, the economy declines because there is less demand for goods and services. At that point the government needs to increase its spending to make up the difference.

It is important to note that Keynesian Economics was starting to be developed while the dollar was coming off of the gold standard. Today our economic system is based on a system of debt, and that changes everything!

Today our government and governments around the world have embraced Keynesian Economics, and that is why they encourage spending. That's one reason the government spends so much. The problem is the debt based system we all find ourselves in will one day implode if America cannot find a way to reduce its debt. The GCR crowd will point to valid issues like this, but in the end you won't receive the whole story. That's the reason for this book.

Many Keynesian fiscal policies are inherently flawed. Some politicians are using the Keynesian approach to permanently expand government! In fact, you will find there are some similarities of Keynesian principles in Das Kapital, which was written in part by "the father of communism" Karl Marx.

The core belief of Keynesian theory is to put more money in people's pockets during a downturn economy. This could be done through government programs, public works, or tax cuts in the form of rebates. Keynesian economics seems to overlook the fact that governments can't inject money into the economy without first taking money out of the economy in the form of taxes and debt. There is no increase to aggregate demand (the total demand for final goods and services in an economy at a given time). The Keynesian philosophy does not boost income. It only redistributes it. The people who lend the money to government are generally not the same people who benefit from the government programs. It shifts money from one part of the economy to another part. The pie is divided up differently, but it is the same size pie.

The Keynesian supporters will say it is better than letting the money sit idle. They seem to overlook the fact that in downturns people tend to save money or pay off debt. So the money is sitting idle anyway. Consumer confidence would need to rise in a bad economy to increase consumer spending.

Government could also print money instead of borrowing or taking it through higher taxes. As we discussed earlier this process could lead to bankrupting the economy. Examples of this can be found by looking at Zimbabwe and Argentina. These economies were ruined due to the overprinting of their currency. Keynesian economics has failed in the real world, too. Let's look at some examples.

During the great depression Herbert Hoover boosted taxes dramatically. This included a boost in the top tax rate from 25 percent to 63 percent. He inserted protectionist policies such as the Smoot-Hawley Tariff Act. This crippled world trade for the U.S. He increased intervention of private markets. He also boosted government spending by 47 percent over a period of 4 years. He financed government spending with debt. So here we see the Keynesian model.

He entered public office with a surplus, but when he left office there was a deficit of 4.5 percent of GDP. He left office with government debt, and the whole time Hoover's approach was followed economic growth went down while unemployment went up. The whole time these policies were put in place the Federal Reserve was contracting the money supply because they believed that his policies would lead to inflation.

Franklin Delano Roosevelt followed the same Keynesian approach. He boosted the top tax rate to 79 percent. Government intervention became more pervasive. More taxes were put on consumer goods while government spending skyrocketed. This policy seemed to punish the poor even more. Government spending rose 106 percent from 1933 to 1940, but the average unemployment rate during the 1930s was 17.2 percent. Overall economic output did not get back to the pre-1929 level until World War II.

In the end, a bigger government limits freedom through government regulations, and it hurts the economy by misallocating economic resources. This produces a vicious cycle as Keynesian economics always produces a larger government that spends more money as a side effect. That's why the Keynesian model doesn't work in real life.

This is not to say that there should be no government regulation. Government regulations need to be put in place in order to protect the consumer, but they should never be designed to stimulate the economy. Through the Keynesian model the government tries to control the growth of the economy through needless regulations and programs, an action that always creates economic turmoil in the end.

The Federal Reserve

In order to properly understand money mechanics we need to understand the role that the Federal Reserve plays. The Federal Reserve is a central bank. What is a central bank? It is a national bank that provides financial and banking services for its country's government, along with services for the commercial banking system. It also implements the government's monetary policy, creates money, and issues currency.

There are many conspiracy theories surrounding the Federal Reserve today. Many people have fallen for these theories in part because it takes a lot of research and work to dig up the truth about this institution, and most people don't have time to do the research. It's easier to believe the conspiracy theories than it is to spend countless hours debunking it. So allow me if you will to lay out the conspiracy theories. Then we will set the record straight. You will find links in the last chapter of this book that will verify the things I say, and will enable you to conduct your own research.

It is widely believed that the Federal Reserve is a private banking institution with no governmental oversight set up by bankers from around the world. These bankers own shares of stock in the Federal Reserve, which is no more a part of the federal government than Federal Express. The name "Federal" is there just to make you think it is part of the government. The Fed sets the nation's monetary policy, but it is really controlled by a global organization known as "The Cabal" (for those who are anti-Semitic) or "The Illuminati" (for those who are anti-Catholic) that uses the U.S. dollar to manipulate U.S. policy around the world. This same global organization buys all the politicians and controls everything. At the head of all of this is the Rothschild family. Since the Rothschild family is really Jewish, the only logical conclusion to this conspiracy is that the Jews own the banking industry. Other families and dynasties played a role as well. For example, J.P. Morgan was supposedly a Rothschild agent and represented their interests.

The formation of the Federal Reserve was also sinister. The 1907 Bankers' Panic was started by J.P. Morgan in an effort to gain control of the banking structure. A group of bankers secretly gathered on Jekyll Island and wrote the legislation. J.P. Morgan organized the whole thing, and it was pushed through congress by their representative Rhode Island Sen. Nelson

Aldrich. They waited until the Christmas holidays to vote on it, and then we are told that while most of congress was at home the legislation was passed by a minority of supporters and President Wilson quickly signed it into law. Many members of congress were opposed to the new banking structure, but the law was already passed when they got back from their Christmas break.

It is further believed by this group of conspiracists that the 16th amendment was never ratified; therefore the current tax system is illegal. All taxes collected go to the private bank known as The Federal Reserve to pay the American debt. This is debt that the Federal Reserve creates when it loans money to the government. The Federal Reserve prints money that is used all over the world, and bankers are acquiring wealth as a result of the interest that has to be paid. The Federal Reserve makes a yearly profit which is then passed on to the rest of the bankers.

This is the total conspiracy theory in a nutshell, although there are several versions of the theory with small variations. It amazes me to see how many people have fallen for this. You'll find this belief at the core of many money conspiracy theories and investment scams. The real truth is much different. Now let's look at the actual events that led to the formation of the Federal Reserve.

The primary reason our central banking system was implemented was because of the free banking systems, the ones that aren't centralized. The free banking era started from Andrew Jackson's administration, and ended during Abraham Lincoln's administration. These banks were extremely unstable. Between 1837 and 1862, a time when America had free banking, banks issued their own currency. These bank notes were backed against their own gold and silver supplies. At the time, states regulated reserve requirements, interest rates on loans and deposits, and many other things the central bank regulates today. The main problem with this system is it created a lot of unstable banks. In fact, banks would only last around 5 years before going bankrupt because they could no longer redeem their notes to precious metals. Customers would withdraw the gold from a bank if they thought the bank's gold supply was low. A third of all banks failed during the free banking era. When federal money laws were introduced during the 1860s it provided some stability, but before the Federal Reserve System the average lifespan of a new bank was still a mere five years!

As we discussed earlier, there was a bankers' panic that occurred in 1907. An investigation was conducted after the banking panic of 1907, and the conclusion was that there were problems with the money supply because it had no elasticity. In other words, the money supply was not easily expanded and contracted as society's needs changed. In the first part of the 20th century an average of 70 banks would fail each year. People wanted a more stable banking structure. By 1910 congress felt a need to find a way to stabilize the banking system. Woodrow Wilson campaigned on banking reform in 1912.

Nelson Aldrich spent time traveling around Europe in 1910. He strongly believed the English, French and German, central banking systems were much better than any banking system the U.S. had at the time. He believed and supported progressive concepts of efficiency and science. He wanted a banking system that worked well and was stable. He worked with various bankers and economists to design a central banking system for America. The truth is he promoted a central banking concept that was decentralized! This makes it hard to believe he was part of any large conspiracy. It was supposed to be a system that gave the central bank power over economic decisions without seeking the approval of congress or the executive branch. The reality is that back in 1910 banking reform was a big issue in the United States. The key meeting place for banking reform took place on Jekyll Island in Georgia. This meeting was really not as secretive as some suggest. We know exactly who attended:

- Charles D Norton (President, First National Bank of New York)
- AP Andrews (Assistant Secretary of the Treasury Department)
- Nelson Aldrich, US Senator
- Paul Warburg (Kuhn, Loeb, & Co)
- Frank A Vanderlip (President, National City Bank of New York)
- Henry P Davison (Senior Partner, JP Morgan Company)
- Benjamin Strong (Representing JP Morgan)

This was not a secret meeting of bankers! A U.S. Senator and the assistant Secretary of the Treasury were also there. Congress and the Department of treasury were represented at this meeting. The whole "secret meeting" mystery can be attributed to Forbes magazine. They published an article several years later about a bunch of bankers skipping town in the middle of the night to some island.

The conspiracists imply that nobody knew about the Federal Reserve Act. The truth is it had been debated and discussed for over 4 months prior to being voted on. It passed the House on December 22, 1913 with 298 "yeas" to 60 "nays". 76 congressmen did not vote, but even if they all voted "nay" it still would have passed by a majority of yeas! The next day the Senate passed the act with 43 "yeas" to 25 "nays". This left 27 senators not voting. However, the record shows that almost all of those not voting on the bill had previously declared their intentions over the time it was debated, and the senators that were absent were paired with members of the opposite intentions creating an equal number. In other words, if every member of the Senate was there to vote it still would have passed!

The charge remains that the Federal Reserve is a private banking institution. However, that is not necessarily true in the U.S. because the Fed must answer to Congress. Since the Federal Reserve is private, Congress cannot control it and use it for political means. This may seem like a contradiction, but it is like a private institution that is indirectly controlled by the US Congress.

Apparently the conspiracists have a very small understanding of the Federal Reserve. Yes it is a private institution; however it is not as private as Federal Express. It is considered private because the decisions it makes do not necessarily have to be ratified by the President or anyone else in the executive branch or congress! The conspiracy theorists ignore the fact that the Federal Reserve has a board of governors with seats for congressional officials. The Federal Reserve is also subject to heavy oversight from Congress. Therefore, it is not necessarily a private or a public entity! Rather, it is "independent within the government"!

Basically, congress passed a law that created a central banking system that is allowed to make monetary policy such as interest rate adjustments without the approval of Congress or the President. These branches of government tend to make policy for political gain, and that is the very reason for the central banking system – to shield their policy decisions from political influence.

Let's clear up some more misconceptions about the central bank. The Federal Reserve is the only institution within government that funds itself. Through the services it provides it makes a healthy profit every year. These profits are in the billions of dollars, and they are mainly generated from interest. The profits are turned over to the United States Government every year! The Federal Reserve does not increasingly create debt due to interest. The Federal Reserve rebates its net earnings to the Treasury every year. Thus, the money borrowed from the Federal Reserve has no net interest obligation for the treasury! A portion of the debt that the United States has accumulated over the years is owed to The Federal Reserve. This institution does not print money! The Fed does not own one printing press that is used for creating paper currency! Money is printed by the United States Treasury. It is then distributed through the Federal Reserve. The Federal Reserve has the power to create money, but the money it creates is electronic.

This just leaves the last part of the conspiracy theory. "The 16th amendment was never ratified, and congress does not have the right to tax the American people." That's actually not true. Congress does indeed have the power to impose an income tax! The Sixteenth Amendment never imposed this tax! It eliminates the requirement that direct income must be apportioned (divided and distributed). Taxes on income from property had always been subjected to indirect taxes. These taxes were not subject to apportionment. The purpose of the 16th Amendment is to make the origin of income irrelevant. This also included physical labor, in regards to the apportionment rule.

This rumor has been on the Internet for a long time. It especially thrives in conspiracy theory circles. The whole thing can be traced to William J. Benson and his book published in1985, *"The Law That Never Was"*. In this book he claims that the 16th Amendment was not properly ratified. In December of 2007 Benson's *"Defense Reliance Package"*, which contained all of his arguments, was sold on the Internet. People purchased his so-called legal argument claiming the 16th Amendment was never ratified when they got in trouble with the IRS.

A federal court ruled it to be a *"fraud perpetrated by Benson that had caused needless confusion and a waste of the customers' and the IRS' time and resources."* Also stated by the court *"Benson has failed to point to evidence that would create a genuinely disputed fact regarding whether the Sixteenth Amendment was properly ratified or whether United States Citizens are legally obligated to pay federal taxes."*

In reality it was ratified by 36 states. One more state ratified it a short time later. This is more than enough for the 3/4ths majority that is required in order to ratify the amendment. There were 48 states at this time and 37 of them are equal to a little over 77 percent. This is more than the 75 percent that is required for an amendment to be ratified.

BRICS and PIIGS

BRICS is the acronym that is associated with five major emerging national economies - Brazil, Russia, India, China, and South Africa. (The acronym was originally known as "BRIC", but South Africa was added back in 2011.) As of 2014, the BRICS nations represented about 18 percent of the world's economy, and they had an estimated $4 trillion in combined foreign reserves, which were mostly U.S. dollars. These economies were strong in 2014, and people felt that they were economies to invest in.

Some of these economies started to decline in 2015, however. The BRICS nations have slowed in their growth and some have reversed course. Brazil and Russia are in full blown recessions, China is trying to stave off a big slowdown, and India, while still of interest to global investors, is struggling to put through the economic reforms required that would help it reach its full potential.

Brazil is the first of the BRICS nations to break down on so many fronts all at once. Russia and South Africa are both in deep crisis, and at one point China was running through $100bn of foreign reserves a month. The BRICS concept has become completely meaningless, but it is still mentioned in conspiracist circles.

PIIGS is an acronym used to describe a certain group of countries that have some amount of similarity in location and economic situations. These countries are Portugal, Ireland, Italy, Greece, and Spain. The term PIGS originated in the 1990s. This term originally referred to the economies of Portugal, Italy, Greece and Spain, but with the rise of the European Sovereign-Debt Crisis, Ireland also became associated with the acronym. These economies all use the euro.

The euro is the currency that represents the Eurozone, and the nations listed above are all members of the Eurozone. Nineteen out of a total of twenty-eight members of the European Union are represented by the euro. Because the debts and the GDP of these nations have been historically bad, each country listed has been a drain on the euro as other member nations had to pick up the tab for their poor economies.

Derivatives

A derivative is a financial contract between two or more parties with a value that is derived and agreed upon from an underlying commodity or asset. Typically derivatives have no direct value in and of themselves. Their value is based primarily on the expected future price movements of their underlying asset in the contract.

A derivative can be based on many things, but the most common derivatives include bonds, commodities, currencies, interest rates, market indices and stocks.

Derivatives are often used as an instrument to hedge risk for one party of a contract, while offering the potential for high returns for the other party. Derivatives have been created to mitigate a remarkable number of risks which include fluctuations in stocks, bonds, and commodities. Other risks can include index prices, weather events, changes in foreign exchange rates, and changes in interest rates. These are just a few of the things that are used to hedge against risk.

One of the most commonly used derivatives is the option. Futures contracts, forward contracts, options, swaps, and warrants are common derivatives. The value of the derivative is determined from the asset that backs it. For example, a stock option is a derivative because its value is "derived" from that of the underlying stock.

Derivatives are used for speculating as well as for hedging risk. Speculators seek to profit from changing prices in the underlying asset, index, or security. Derivatives that are used as a hedge allow the risks associated with the underlying asset's price to be transferred between the parties involved in the contract.

Many people in these monetary conspiracy theory circles view derivatives as money or debt. They tend to view them as a deceitful way of expanding the money supply. This is simply not the case. Derivatives are not limited to currency, and their primary function is to place value on commodities or assets. This is why the global derivative market is so large.

I hope that this was not too painful for you. We need to be familiar with financial mechanics and terminology as we proceed in our quest to understand the Global Currency Reset. Now let's look further into what actually happened during the meltdown of 2008. This event prompted the call for a new currency to replace the dollar.

Chapter Seven- the 2008 Meltdown

Let us retrace the steps that led to the meltdown that occurred in 2008. Understanding this financial crisis is pivotal to understanding the mentality behind the Global Currency Reset theory. After the meltdown the currency wars began. Everything has really been a series of dominos; when one domino falls it hits another, tipping it over as well. Let's go back to the beginning of this whole mess.

In the 1980s investment banks went public. This brought major money to the markets for investing. Deregulation of the savings and loans institutions in 1982 led to bad investments. The Depository Institutions Deregulation and Monetary Control Act of 1980 and the Garn–St. Germain Depository Institutions Act of 1982 created the path to deregulation. The deregulation not only allowed thrifts to offer a wider array of savings products, but also significantly expanded their lending authority. They began to invest in real estate ventures. Most of these investments were designed to be tax write-offs. This led to a real estate boom in the early part of the 1980s.

The Tax Reform Act of 1986 significantly decreased the value of many such investments, which were held more for their tax-advantaged status than for their inherent profitability. This contributed to the end of the real estate boom of the early to mid-1980s, and facilitated the savings and loan crisis.

Prior to 1986, passive investors did much of the real estate investing. It was common for syndicates of investors to pool their resources in order to invest in property. This applied to commercial or residential properties. They would then hire management companies to run the operation.

TRA 86 reduced the value of these investments by limiting the extent to which losses associated with them could be deducted from the investor's gross income. This, in turn, encouraged the holders of loss-generating properties to try to unload them, which contributed further to the problem of sinking real estate values.

In the 1980s Frank Keating ran American Continental Corporation and the Lincoln Savings and Loan Association. He took advantage of loosened restrictions on banking investments, and his enterprises began to suffer financial problems which led to investigations by federal regulators.

His association with five U.S. senators due to campaign contributions brought help from these senators, who argued for preferential treatment from the regulators. That led to them being dubbed "The Keating Five". When Lincoln S&L failed in 1989 it cost the federal government over $3 billion, and about 23,000 customers were left with worthless bonds.

Deregulation continued during the Clinton administration. Larry Summers served as the U.S. Secretary of the Treasury between 1999 and 2001 under Clinton. During this time he was most noted for his support in getting the Gramm-Leach-Bliley Act through congress. This repealed the Glass-Steagall Act that passed in 1933 after the Great Depression started. The Glass-Steagall Act put limits on what banks could do. This was the final capstone in removing all regulation from the bankers.

This helped pave the way for the market manipulation to come, as big banks that emerged in the late 1990s now pulled the strings. In 1998 Citigroup merged with Travelers to form Citicorp. This was illegal under the Glass-Steagall Act, but they were given a year pass until the Gram-Leach Bliley bill could be passed into law. This act is also known as the Financial Services Modernization Act. By the end of the Clinton administration there were major players and monopolies emerging in the banking industry.

Once total deregulation was accomplished, investment banks came up with a new group of products known as derivatives. Larry Summers (Director of the National Economic Council) and Alan Greenspan (Chairman of the Federal Reserve) fought the regulation of derivatives. Brooksley Born (chairperson of the Commodity Futures Trading Commission) tried to regulate the market. Larry Summers and Alan Greenspan shut her down with the aid of Congress. The Commodity Futures Modernization Act shut down any regulation. By 2003 derivatives in the U.S. had become a global $56 trillion market!

By the time George W. Bush took office there was a major financial powerhouse in play. There were two financial conglomerates (Citicorp, J.P. Morgan). There were three Insurance Securities companies (AIG, MBIA, and AMBAC). There were five major investment banks (Goldman Sachs, Morgan Stanley, Lehman Brothers, Bear Stearns, and Merrill Lynch). There were three rating agencies (Moody's, Fitch, and Standard and Poor's).

A Securitization Food Chain Linked Everything Together

HOME BUYERS--MORTGAGE LENDERS--INVESTMENT BANKS--INVESTORS.

Before deregulation, mortgage banks made loans for housing and people paid the lender back. Because the bank would be on the hook for the loan, they were very careful about issuing loans and who was receiving the loan.

After deregulation and under the new system mortgages were sold to investment banks. Investment banks then sold these loans to investors. Commercial mortgages, corporate buyout debt, home mortgages, car loans, student loans, and credit card debt all combined to create something called Collateralized Debt Obligations (or "CDOs"). Investment banks sold these CDOs to investors all over the world. The investment banks paid the three rating agencies to rate the loans. CDOs were given a triple A rating (AAA), the highest rating available. They got these ratings because security insurance companies like AIG insured all CDOs.

Because investment banks sold these CDOs to investors, now when you paid your mortgage it bypassed the lender and the investment bank and your payment went straight to the investor. Since mortgage companies were no longer on the hook for the loans they granted, anyone could get a loan. Since investment banks needed CDOs to sell to investors in order to make profits, all debt regardless of risk was welcome. The loan industry did not care who received the loans that constructed these CDO investments.

The rating companies received money to rate these CDOs. They were paid by the investment banks. Since retirement accounts like 401k, 401b and pension funds could only hold securities with the highest rating, a lot of CDOs made their way into these retirement funds. Predatory lending became a common practice to produce even more CDOs for an ever-growing market demand.

As a result, most CDOs became junk investments. The main buyers of these junk investments were the low risk money market accounts, 401k, 401b, pension funds, and other retirement accounts. Even though the CDOs were insured, they were very risky.

The problem was, anyone could take a policy out for any CDO they wished. That meant that companies like AIG would make higher profits from premiums made on the same CDO. You could not have 20 people insure the same house, but you could have 20 people insure the same CDO. This created a market manipulation that valued some CDOs higher than others. Certain junk CDOs started trading with a higher value. Some of the investment banks knew that the bulk of these CDOs were junk.

On October 14, 2004 the New York State Office of Attorney General Eliot Spitzer announced that it had commenced a civil action against Marsh & McLennan Companies for steering clients to preferred insurers with whom the company maintained lucrative payoff agreements, and for soliciting rigged bids for insurance contracts from the insurers. The Attorney General announced in a release that two AIG executives pleaded guilty to criminal charges in connection with this illegal course of conduct. In early May 2005, AIG restated its financial position and issued a reduction in book value of USD $2.7 billion, a 3.3 percent reduction in net worth. On February 9, 2006 AIG and the New York State Attorney General's office agreed to a settlement in which AIG would pay a fine of $1.6 billion.

In 2007 the housing market began to show signs of cracks. Predatory lending was beginning to come back and haunt the industry. In 2008 everything began to collapse. The whole economy began to melt down, due in part to the debt and predatory lending that made its way into the stock market.

Higher gas prices fueled the fire, creating a domino effect almost as if someone was orchestrating this from behind the scenes. Oil sold for over $148 a barrel. As a result, gas prices skyrocketed to over $5.00 a gallon in some states. The higher gas prices also meant that it cost more to bring goods to market. In many areas of the country the cost for food doubled. The general cost of living rose as inflation began to set in. These events caused many more people to default on their mortgages.

Bear Sterns completely failed. Then in September of 2008 the major investment bank Lehman Brothers filed bankruptcy. Bankruptcy laws are different around the world, and the global corporations that failed had different global impact. In London, Lehman had to completely close its doors the very day it filed bankruptcy. Jobs in England immediately vanished.

By the time the dust cleared fifty million people fell below the poverty line. Thirty million people were now unemployed. Lehman Brothers was gone, Bank of America purchased Merrill Lynch, and J.P. Morgan-Chase purchased Bear Stearns. Bankruptcies in 2008 shot up 32 percent from the previous year. Wealth and money vanished as debt was removed from the books. Retirement accounts like 401k and 401b lost a lot of money due to the fact that they held many of these junk CDOs. The greatest recession to ever hit America was now in full swing.

A lot of the expanded money supply vanished because of this crash. As debts were canceled through bankruptcies and housing markets adjusted their perceived values, the money supply drastically fell. CDOs were really nothing but debt, and because most of these so-called assets were junk, the markets adjusted accordingly.

In the fall of 2008 oil fell drastically. Its high for the year was over $149 a barrel on the global market. In the fall the price dropped and fluctuated in the $40 to $50 a barrel range. The high oil prices contributed greatly to the harshness of the initial collapse. As fuel prices rose sharply the cost of delivering these goods to market was passed on to consumers. Victims of predatory lending could no longer pay their debts due to the overall inflation brought on by higher oil prices. To add insult to injury, credit was severely tightened, creating an even harder environment for recovery.

Government's Role

I have just explained the mechanism that was created and I went into detail about how everything came crashing down, but this story is not complete. Many conspiracists and liberals and even some conservatives have blamed the banking industry. The truth is the government is primarily responsible for the meltdown that took place. The banking industry was reacting to government laws and regulations. Many of the lending institutions were forced into the position of careless lending as fears about discrimination were being hammered out through government threats and legislation.

As we already discussed when we described the effects of Keynesian Economics, whenever our government gets involved with the economy in an effort to stimulate growth through redistribution they are asking for trouble. Let me explain the government's role in the 2008 meltdown.

The Federal National Mortgage Association, commonly referred to as Fannie Mae or FNMA, is a government-sponsored enterprise otherwise known as a GSE. Fannie May has been a publicly traded company since 1968. It was founded in 1938 during the Great Depression as part of FDR's New Deal. The purpose of this corporation is to expand the secondary mortgage market by making mortgages more secure in the form of mortgage-backed securities or MBS. These mortgage-backed securities allow lenders to reinvest their assets into more lending. It increases the number of lenders in the mortgage market by reducing the reliance on locally based savings and loan associations

The Federal Home Loan Mortgage Corporation, also known as Freddie Mac (FHLMC), is a public government-sponsored enterprise or GSE. They are headquartered in the Tyson's Corner CDP in unincorporated Fairfax County, Virginia. The FHLMC was created in 1970 to expand the secondary market for mortgages in the U.S. Along with Fannie Mae, Freddie Mac buys mortgages on the secondary market, pools them together, and then sells them as a mortgage-backed security to investors on the open market. This secondary mortgage market increases the supply of money available for mortgage lending, and it increases the money available for new home purchases.

Barney Frank is a former American politician and board member of the New York-based Signature Bank. He previously served as a member of the U.S. House of Representatives from Massachusetts from 1981 to 2013 as a member of the Democratic Party. He also served as chairman of the House Financial Services Committee, which has jurisdiction over issues pertaining to the economy, the banking system, housing, insurance, and securities and exchanges. It oversees Fannie and Freddie.

Frank was criticized by conservative organizations for receiving campaign contributions totaling $42,350 between 1989 and 2008. News organizations claimed the donations from Fannie and Freddie influenced his support of their lending programs. These claims said that Frank did not play a strong enough role in reforming the institutions in the years leading up to the economic crisis of 2008. In 2006 a Fannie Mae representative stated in SEC filings that they *"did not participate in large amounts of these non-traditional mortgages in 2004 and 2005."* In response to criticism, Frank said, *"In 2004, it was Bush who started to push Fannie and Freddie into subprime mortgages, because they were boasting about how they were expanding homeownership for low-income people. And I said at the time, 'Hey—(a) this is going to jeopardize their profitability, but (b) it's going to put people in homes they can't afford, and they're gonna lose them."*

According to a Fox News report that aired on September 24th 2008, many financial experts claim that if Fannie Mae and Freddie Mac were regulated years ago, the subprime mortgage meltdown would have never happened. The Bush administration raised red flags in April of 2001. During the 2002 budget request the Bush administration called both Freddie Mac and Fannie Mae a potential problem. In 2003 the Bush administration gave another warning about the two mortgage giants, and upgraded the warning to a systemic risk that could spread beyond the housing sector. By the fall of 2003 the Bush administration was pushing Congress hard to create a new federal agency that would regulate and supervise Fannie Mae and Freddie Mac. At that time Treasury Secretary John Snow was getting a lot of pushback from Barney Frank. Congressman Frank claimed that the U.S. should do more to get low income families into housing. The legislation was blocked by Democrats.

Shortly after, Alan Greenspan made the claim that the entire financial system is being placed at risk as Fannie and Freddie increase in size. He said later on this topic "if we fail to strengthen GSC regulation, we increase the possibility of insolvency and crisis." The two mortgage giants had big defenders. Charles Schumer later came to their defense. John McCain tried to issue legislation that would regulate the two mortgage giants in May of 2006. That bill made it out of the Senate Banking Committee with all the Democrats voting against it. Although some Republicans tried to regulate the mortgage industry, their efforts were blocked by a consensus in the Democratic Party. Then by the middle of 2007 it was too late as the whole system started to crash.

Of course we find that Congressman Frank blamed the financial crisis on the failure to adequately regulate the banks, blaming others for his own mistakes. Barney Frank pursued a course of using the government's authority to force lower underwriting standards in the business of housing finance. He did this for most of his career. Now he claims he tried to reverse course in 2003, the year that he made the often quoted remark, *"I want to roll the dice a little bit more in this situation toward subsidized housing."* Instead of reversing course like he claims, he was pursuing his course of action when others were warning congress of the potential outcome.

Congressman Frank imposed what were called "affordable housing" requirements on Fannie Mae and Freddie Mac back in 1992. Before these regulations these two GSEs had been required to buy only mortgages that institutional investors would buy. Only prime mortgages were purchased by the two giants. However, Frank and his cohorts thought these standards made it too hard for low income borrowers to buy homes. Because of this, affordable housing laws required Fannie and Freddie to meet government quotas when they purchased loans from banks and other mortgage institutions.

This quota started out being 30 percent. This meant that of all the loans they purchased, 30 percent had to be made to people at or below the median income in their communities. The authority to administer these quotas was given to HUD. Between the years 1992 and 2007 the quotas were raised. They went from 30 percent to 50 percent under Clinton. They were raised again to 55 percent under Bush.

By 2000, Fannie was offering no down payment loans. By 2002, Fannie and Freddie had purchased well over one trillion dollars in subprime and other high risk, low quality loans. Fannie and Freddie were by far the largest part of this effort. The Veterans Administration, FHA, Federal Home Loan Banks, and other agencies followed the same practice. They were all under congressional and HUD pressure to do so. The practice continued through the 1990s and 2000s until the housing bubble began to collapse in 2007 as a result of all of this government-backed spending.

Before the mortgage meltdown which triggered the crisis that occurred in 2008, there were 27 million subprime and other low quality mortgages in the US financial system. That was a little over half of all mortgages. Of these, over 70 percent or 19.2 million were on the books of government agencies like Fannie Mae and Freddie Mac! Housing prices rose by an artificial demand as many people received loans for which they would not normally qualify. There is no doubt whatsoever that the government created the very demand for these weak loans! Less than 30 percent or 7.8 million were held by the banks! They profited from the opportunity created by the government. When these mortgages failed in unprecedented numbers in 2008, they weakened all financial institutions and caused the financial crisis. As a result housing prices were driven down throughout the U.S.

Congressman Frank makes wild claims about who was ultimately responsible, but he has no data to back up his claims. Many other government officials hold his position in an effort to shift blame. He says that the banks were responsible, but there is no way he can dispute the numbers or give an account for the number of subprime mortgages that Fannie and Freddie held at the time. These numbers show beyond any reasonable doubt that it was the government's housing policy that caused the financial crisis! He has even confessed that government was the problem. In an interview on Larry Kudlow's show in August 2010, he said *"I hope by next year we'll have abolished Fannie and Freddie ... it was a great mistake to push lower-income people into housing they couldn't afford and couldn't really handle once they had it."*

Those who took advantage of the opportunity offered by the government's policies are not to blame for the crisis. It is the government's fault for offering a housing finance program without making any effort to prevent the deterioration in mortgage underwriting standards. You can't just blame those who make use of government programs. They are not responsible for the government's lack of oversight or the current national debt.

In 2008 Fannie Mae went under government supervision. In August 2009 Fannie published the first credit report on its mortgage exposures. This report showed that 81 percent of Fannie's 2008 losses had come from its exposure to both subprime loans and other loans that were particularly risky because they had low or no down payments. On most of these subprime loans the borrower had a FICO credit score of 660 or lower! Further inquiry would have shown that Freddie Mac had suffered similar losses for the same reasons.

Because Fannie and Freddie were the dominant players in the housing finance market, when they reduced their underwriting standards lenders were compelled to do the same. Mortgage lending is very competitive, and consumers went to the lenders that offered the easiest terms and the best conditions. Hindsight shows why Countrywide ultimately became one of the largest mortgage originators in the U.S. It was one of the principal suppliers to Fannie and

Freddie, who bought all those subprime loans for profit or market share. The government's role and the affordable housing goals that drove down underwriting standards were conveniently ignored!

The Dollar is the World's Reserve Currency

The reason why we need to learn about the 2008 meltdown is because it is misrepresented in many of the GCR forums and groups. Many claim that the 2008 meltdown happened because the currency supply expanded too much and it brought down the entire economy. As you just read in this chapter nothing could be further from the truth. The 2008 melt down is also the birthplace of many conspiracy theories and many who claim to have an extensive knowledge about economics also claim to have navigated this 2008 meltdown unscathed.

Most of the self-proclaimed gurus that keep predicting the downfall of the U.S. dollar will also cite 2008 as a sign of the coming currency collapse and the reason to buy whatever they are selling. As of this writing, the U.S. dollar is still the main reserve currency used throughout the world, thanks to this petrodollar system. But that could very well change. There has been an international cry for a new reserve currency since the 2008 meltdown.

Today we have an out of control debt, and a reduction in the U.S. credit rating. The funny thing here is that the credit rating agencies that gave the CDOs a triple A rating are the exact same rating agencies that adjusted the United States credit rating! It should be evident at this point that you can't trust these rating agencies.

All of this only served to fuel the rumors of a coming global currency reset.

Chapter Eight - Iraq and the Dinar

The United States vigorously defends the petrodollar system because it gives the dollar tremendous value and it keeps our economy going. The United States has remained a leader in global affairs because of the petrodollar system. This can explain why certain events happen throughout the world.

Iraq has played a role in the petrodollar system as well. In 1990, Iraq invaded Kuwait. Because of the petrodollar agreement, the United States had to come to Kuwait's defense. For some strange reason this surprised Iraq. Iraq also exported oil under some of the same petrodollar agreements. Up until this time, America gave aid to Iraq due to its ongoing war with Iran.

If America did not defend Kuwait then the petrodollar system would be in danger of collapsing around the world. America really had no choice, and Saudi Arabia was used as a base for operations. After the first gulf war Iraq had sanctions placed on them. Saddam was still in power at this point.

Because of these sanctions Iraq had to find a way to print their own currency, so China printed dinar for Iraq to use. Saddam kept printing new money after the first gulf war through China, but the bills were very poor in quality. The paper was thin and it tore easily. The ink ran on many of these notes. It was hard to tell the difference between the poorly made new Saddam notes and the fake counterfeit Iraqi notes that began to circulate. These new notes became known as "military notes." Few people, least of all speculators, wanted anything to do with them.

The prewar 25-dinar bill became the preferred note. They became known as Swiss dinars because they were printed in Switzerland by De La Rue. No one wanted the new notes because they were easy to counterfeit. Saddam began to conduct foreign trade using the Swiss dinar. Countries like Jordan and Syria conducted trade with Iraq using these notes. They did this because they were told that the Swiss dinar would greatly increase in value after sanctions on Iraq were lifted. Billions of Swiss dinars were used in trade, and speculators wanted the notes as an investment.

Many Jordanian businessmen accepted Iraqi currency for payment. In many cases, these were payments made directly from the Iraqi Government. Once these exchanges were made the Swiss dinar was stashed away. Families mortgaged their homes, shepherds sold their sheep, people sold their gold jewelry, and many withdrew their savings. All of this activity was done to buy the Swiss dinar.

Many Jordanian people supported Iraq after the Gulf War. While most people outside the Arab world couldn't understand why a stack of Iraqi banknotes with Saddam's mug on the front seemed like a sound investment, many Jordanians believed and were even told by leaders in Iraq that the United Nations embargo against Iraq would one day be lifted. They believed that the Swiss dinar would regain its old value once Baghdad resumed its oil sales. Iraq conducted trade using these notes with its neighbors many months after the war.

As the old Swiss 25-dinar notes began to disappear from Iraq, inflation soared. The Iraqi government kept getting more bills from China.

In May of 1993, Iraqi monetary officials invalidated the Swiss dinar notes. This one move quickly removed an estimated 25 billion dinars from circulation.

Iraqis were permitted to exchange the 25-dinar notes for the new currency, but they closed the borders for six days to keep speculators outside the country from exchanging. The border was reopened on a Tuesday, after the Monday deadline to turn in the old notes passed. Iraqi officials had no intention of compensating anyone else, even the Jordanian businessmen they traded with lost their investments.

The Kurds were not allowed to trade in their Swiss dinar notes during the exchange process. The old 25-dinar notes continued to circulate among the Kurds even though they were not considered valid currency by the Iraqi government.

In 2000 Saddam switched from selling Iraqi oil in dollars to selling oil in euros. America started to make invasion plans after Saddam made this switch. To be fair, there was intel that suggested that Saddam had some of these chemical WMD. People were afraid that those weapons would end up making their way to America, and WMD was the excuse used to go to war in Iraq. But the threat that Saddam posed to the petrodollar system could not be ignored.

In the fall of 2002 it became more and more likely that the United States would invade. Because of this, the Swiss dinar became more and more valuable. By this time, the other nations that held the Swiss dinar already disposed of it. Twenty-five billion dinar from outside Iraq's border were gone and already destroyed.

Once the United States got control of Iraq, the first order of business was to switch the sale of

Iraqi oil from euros back to dollars. In the rebuilding process, the central bank became a part of Iraq's new constitution. It would be separate from the government. Iraq would rely on the United States dollar as a reserve to back their currency. This would help insure that Iraq would continue to sell oil only using USD. Today 93 percent of Iraq's reserves are US dollars. The other 7 percent is gold. Iraq sold off the euros they had and exchanged them for gold.

In 2003, Iraq went through a redenomination. Old notes with Saddam's picture were pulled from circulation and new dinar (the IQD) was put into circulation. The Swiss dinar that the Kurds used got a higher trade-in value because it could be proven to be authentic.

A new system was set up that allowed the dinar to be exported and sold around the world. In 2004 currency dealers began to spring up selling the new dinar notes along with other currencies. Banks around the world exchanged the new dinar currency until the end of 2011.

Currency groups emerged that speculated on the dinar with a promise that the currency will soon revalue. (Does this sound familiar?) Other currencies like China's yuan and Vietnam's dong are also included in the speculation and sold along with the Iraqi dinar.

There are independent groups that rise up to hype the dinar with the promise that it will gain tremendous value overnight. The spokesmen for these groups become known as gurus because they give the impression of being all-knowing when it comes to currencies and economics. They declare the imminent revaluation of the dinar and pump the sale of the currency. They work with currency dealers from all over the globe. People who never had investments in their lives begin to invest in this currency with the hope of newfound wealth. These people are the target for dinar sales around the world.

In addition to the dinar these dealers start selling a host of other currencies with the promise of a revaluation. The problem is all these currencies that are sold by dealers are overprinted. This is done in an effort to keep the currency value low. People believe in a coming revalue (or "RV") because of junk economics taught in a community of forums. The whole dinar community becomes a subculture. They are taught things about economics that are not true, and the understanding of how money actually works becomes warped and distorted.

As the gurus pump these overprinted currencies we go through the 2008 meltdown. Around 2010 these currency gurus begin to tie the dinar investment to a global currency reset. They get this idea from precious metals merchants and conspiracy theory websites. This idea catches on and many currency dealers tie the RV of overprinted currencies around the world to a coming GCR.

The fact that an event like a massive revalue of currency has never happened before in human history is brushed aside, because everything people know about economics is supposedly wrong. America will be the only country that gets punished for having too much currency, and every other overprinted currency will rise dramatically in value as countries begin to base their currencies' values on their assets or natural resources. These are the conspiracy theories that sell the dinar today!

There is no way that this Iraqi dinar can possibly revalue and make every investor a multi-millionaire overnight. The junk economics taught in some of these forums base everything on wild conspiracy theories and lies. They rewrite history and claim that Kuwait went through a revalue after the Gulf War. They say the same thing about Germany after World War II. The claim is made that people became wealthy because of these events. Even current news events are often twisted and tied to the revaluation of the dinar. Money doesn't work like this, and yet these are the ideas that people are sold.

People who have no background in economics buy into this get-rich-quick scheme hook, line, and sinker. Once they fall for it, they are reeled in like a fish to be gutted for every dollar they have. The dinar quickly becomes a "sure thing". People begin to overleverage and sell everything they own to buy dinar. I have witnessed this first hand on many occasions. Let me explain why this revaluation will not happen.

As of this writing there's a total of over 70 trillion dinar in Iraq's M1 money supply. Most of this is paper. Over 40 trillion of it is outside of the banking system. To put that in perspective, America has a little over 13 trillion in its M2 money supply. There are not enough American dollars to pay for any significant revaluation.

Even though there is more than 40 trillion dinar that remains outside of banks, well over 30 trillion of that amount is outside the borders of Iraq and is held by private investors and speculators. This is why there has not been massive inflation in Iraq due to the currency levels. The bulk of this currency is not in circulation in Iraq.

It is said that Iraq's currency is pegged. While it is classified as a pegged currency, it is in fact a tightly managed float, also known as a dirty float. The "peg" is maintained by the central bank's management of the money supply and foreign currency reserves. In effect, all currencies are either free-floating currencies or managed floats. As stated in the previous chapter, a floating currency means the market determines its value. A managed float means the central bank controls the value. These types of managed floats are often referred to as pegs in the currency forums because that's the official classification.

A revalue will only happen to currencies that the central bank controls. Floating currencies driven by markets do not revalue because the market determines the value. Currency values that are managed by the central bank will revalue as they see fit. Usually revalues happen to control inflation and keep it in check.

Normally central banks decrease the value of the currency as more currency is printed and released into circulation. This was not the case with the dinar.

The idea being sold is that this overprinted currency is going to greatly revalue overnight, creating a host of new millionaires from the people that have invested in it. The same thing is being said about the Vietnamese dong. The speculation is that the Iraqi dinar will revalue anywhere from 1 dollar to 3 dollars. In January of 2012 the exchange rate was 1166 dinar to 1 United States dollar, but since December of 2015 the rate has been 1182:1.

In all of history, there was never a revalue of any currency above 50 percent. In fact, the biggest one I can remember is Singapore. In the springtime of 2010, Singapore's currency revalued 22 percent. The value of the Iraqi dinar in 2012 was 1,170 dinar to one United States dollar. For the dinar to revalue to 1 penny would be a little over a 1,000 percent revalue. For the dinar to revalue to 1 dollar would be a 100,000 percent revalue. For the dinar to go to 3 dollars like many gurus claim would be a 300,000 percent currency revalue. Currencies don't do that. They NEVER work like this!

If a currency revalued to this degree, instead of correcting inflation this action would bring hyperinflation. This would have the same effect as dumping massive amounts of money in the general currency supply. It would totally debase the currency, thus destroying it.

In the past Iraq has planned a redenomination, which the central bank keeps putting off. The language of the redenomination is getting confused with revaluation, and so people believe that Iraq is going to revalue their currency. Because of this hype and belief, massive demand for Iraq's currency is produced throughout the world. People believe they are going to become millionaires overnight. This is why there is over 30 trillion dinar outside of Iraq's borders today. This currency is exported all over the globe. First-time investors from around the world buy dinar with the hope of a financial windfall.

Most of the people who buy these currencies know little about economics. Some have fallen on hard times, and they fall prey to this get-rich-quick scheme. It quickly becomes their only hope, and they become emotionally attached. All of these same conditions apply to the dong or any other currency unit these gurus like to hype.

It is interesting to note that between 2009 and 2014 Iraq has released over 15 trillion dinar. The money outside of the Iraqi banks in 2009 was 21 trillion, 776 billion. In 2014, that number was over 36 trillion. Approximately 15 trillion dinar was released to the general public in just 5 years, and yet Iraq has experienced little inflation. In addition, their exchange rate is not adjusted to reflect the amount of currency released. In fact, their exchange went from 1170 = 1 dollar to 1166 = 1 dollar. It went up 4 pips during this period.

This does not make sense. That amount of currency released among 35 million people would be expected to bring hyperinflation with a downward adjustment of the controlled valuation. Only one thing can explain this. Their currency is being exported! In fact, a massive amount of currency is being exported.

Even when I present the case as to why this RV is impossible, people are reluctant to believe me. When I present the reasons why this can't happen the facts do not seem to matter. Even though this has never, EVER happened in history, people believe that it will happen in the near future.

They believe this dinar will revalue because they believe in a coming global currency reset. In this scenario it doesn't matter what story history has told us. It doesn't matter how currency really works. Economic laws are completely ignored! People honestly believe that every currency around the world will reset in value and all economic laws and principles governing currency are going to change. That is the hype that the GCR movement is selling.

Many people believe that new values will be placed on these currencies through the International Monetary Fund. They believe that the new values of all currencies are calculated by the assets that each nation has. They believe that the dollar will become worthless, and that it will no longer be used as a reserve currency. They believe that this will happen in one night, and it will take the world by surprise. Let's explore this further and look into the origins of the global currency reset.

Chapter Nine - The Aftermath

After 2008, a lot of wealth was lost due to a reduction of values in the housing market, which also had major global impact. To make matters worse the United States now had a struggling economy, and some sort of recovery was desperately needed. Over time, the interest rates were lowered and we went into QE.

The Federal Reserve started buying $600 billion in mortgage-backed securities, and by March 2009 it held $1.75 trillion of bank debt and mortgage-backed securities. It acquired this debt by expanding more base money by purchasing the securities. The money the Federal Reserve started to create began to make up for the amount of money that was lost due to debt monetization. In other words, the amount of expanded money supply lost due to the 2008 collapse and fractional reserve banking was being made up by expanding the monetary base.

At the time, the perception was that this QE policy would also have the added impact of lowering the dollar's value. This brought resentment from nations like China, Russia, India, and Brazil because as our dollar decreases in value, it would theoretically level the playing field and lower the price for U.S. exports. At the same time it would raise the export costs for these nations. America's imports would now cost more because of decreasing dollar values.

The cost of exports was beginning to rise in other countries, and as a result of the 2008 meltdown the currency wars began. They thought they would lose some of their export advantage due to an ever-weakening dollar, and exporting was the strength of their economies. Their global economies already took a beating in 2008 due to the global impact of the meltdown, and now the U.S. was increasing their currency supply. Many saw this further debasement as weakening the dollar abroad.

So as a result, China begins to call for a new reserve currency to replace the dollar. The only problem with this plan is that at this point there doesn't seem to be anything out there that could replace the dollar. Even though the dollar weakened, it is still the strongest currency globally speaking. In addition, in the years since the 2008 meltdown the dollar has actually recovered and strengthened.

Despite everyone's expectations, the U.S. dollar's position as the world's dominant reserve currency became stronger rather than weaker because of the 2008 crisis, and the world became even more dependent on the dollar than it had been prior to the crisis.

The world is stuck into buying dollars because the USD market is huge, liquid, and reliable! It has become a safe haven for countries everywhere. America is caught in a dependence on cheap credit, and because of foreign demand for the dollar America is allowed to spend well beyond its means.

In addition, the United States accumulated a lot of government debt, which allowed the Federal Reserve to begin flooding the global financial system with dollars. As we have learned in previous chapters, the more dollars there are out there, the less value they should have. However, the exact opposite happened. If anything, the dollar has gained slightly in value.

One reason for this is because a huge amount of dollars did not make its way into America's general circulation. Instead, over the past few years these dollars found their way into reserves where they are used to strengthen currencies and economies for other nations all over the globe.

A lot of this happened during a time when the euro had its own difficulties. As a 2010 audit of the Federal Reserve revealed, the dollar even provided help during the European Sovereign-Debt Crisis. The truth is there were no good substitutes for the dollar at that time! If the Federal Reserve followed the same line of thinking that it followed during the Great Depression the dollar would have suffered greatly. Quantitative Easing actually saved the dollar! By expanding the money supply the Federal Reserve made more dollars available for other nations to use. This was at a time when the euro was going through its own crisis. This caused the U.S. dollar to gain strength and gain value overseas. 2014 was the best year for the dollar since 2005, years before the 2008 meltdown when the economy was doing well.

China still insists that the world's reserve still needs to change, and that it should no longer be the dollar alone. Now a call has emerged to use the International Monetary Fund's "Special Drawing Rights" (or "SDRs") as the new international currency. You can think of SDRs as an artificial currency used by the IMF that is defined as a "basket of national currencies". SDRs are allocated by the IMF to its member countries, and are backed by the full faith and credit of the member nations. The IMF uses SDRs for internal accounting purposes.

An SDR is an international type of monetary reserve currency that was created by the IMF in 1969. Its purpose is to operate as a supplement to the existing reserves of member countries. It was created in response to concerns about the limitations of gold and dollars as the sole means of settling international accounts under Bretton Woods. SDRs are designed to augment international liquidity by supplementing the standard reserve currencies. Now there was debate as to whether or not SDRs should replace the U.S. dollar as a reserve altogether.

All of these events of the first decade of the new millennium have become mixed with speculation and wild conspiracy theories that say the dollar is going to crash overnight. The theories claim that the IMF is calling for a global currency reset. Some people who represent gold and silver have claimed that this GCR event will be announced sometime during the first quarter of 2014. Well as you know, there has been no announcement of said event. Later these same people adjusted their claim and said it would happen at the end of the second quarter.

Many people advocate using gold or silver as a protection against the GCR event. Gold and silver sellers/gurus have jumped on this GCR theory by exaggerating a crash in the dollar, and they've been urging people to buy gold and silver not as an investment or asset, but rather as a security against the dollar and as a hedge of protection because of the coming GCR event. The date for this overnight crash has moved several times in the past, and has been predicted many times over. The hype has the effect of selling more foreign currency, gold, and silver.

A subculture of "end of the world" doomsday preachers declare a coming global currency reset based on nothing more than conjecture and wild conspiracy theories blended with real economic issues in an effort to make the whole scenario seem more plausible. Then they predict an overnight dollar crash. The leaders of this subculture then sell products through the use of fear. They have made preppers out of many people, selling things like newsletters, food dehydrators, inside stock tips, gold, silver, and a host of other products. Fear of this overnight dollar crash and the so-called global currency reset moves the products.

Currency dealers and dinar gurus have taken this a step further by saying that the GCR event will bring a revalue of currencies like the dinar and dong. The claim is that when the dollar finally crashes overnight you will see new values placed on these other currencies as they will no longer be backed by the dollar. Instead they will be backed by the resources the nation is able to produce.

There are various conspiracy theories and different definitions for the GCR event, so can you see why it would be hard to separate fact from fiction? After all, China really has called for a replacement to the U.S. dollar. I hope you can see why people get confused about what parts of this whole dollar crash scenario are real. A subtle trick is to take truth and mix it with deception, making the lies seem more plausible. This is what really makes the GCR event seem more real.

The first observation GCR people make is that the United States got in this mess in part by over printing their currency. If that is indeed the case then another overprinted currency is not going to replace the dollar. Here are the amounts of currencies some of these nations have at their disposal as of this writing. (2016)

China – 151 trillion Yuan
Iraq – 86.6 trillion Dinars
Russia – 36.6 trillion Rubles
India – 27.7 trillion Rupees
Vietnam – 5,179.9 trillion Dong
Euro zone – 10.5 trillion Euros (M2)

Now compare that with the U.S. Dollar, which is 13 Trillion! (M2)

Can someone please tell me why any of these other countries with over inflated currencies will replace the dollar? After all, they seem to have the same problem finding the off switch to their printers! The truth is the dollar has gained strength since the 2008 meltdown, despite the fact that virtually everyone expected the exact opposite!

If currencies are going to be based solely on a nation's resources, then maybe people should understand how many different resources the United States has. Let's review just a few of these resources,

- The United States had 8.73 trillion cubic meters of natural gas in their proven reserves as of January 1, 2013.
- The United states was ranked 5th in the world for proven oil reserves in 2011. The amount given in this estimate is 26.5 billion barrels.
- The United States maintains a Strategic Petroleum Reserve at four sites in the Gulf of Mexico, with a total capacity of 727 million barrels of crude oil. The maximum total withdrawal capability from the United States Strategic Petroleum Reserve is 4.4 million barrels per day. This is roughly 32% of US oil imports, or 75% of imports from OPEC.

- Services under the U.S. Department of the Interior estimate the total volume of undiscovered, technically recoverable oil in the United States to be roughly 134 billion barrels. The Minerals Management Service (MMS) estimates the Federal Outer Continental Shelf (OCS) contains between 66.6 and 115.1 billion barrels of undiscovered technically recoverable crude oil.
- The Gulf of Mexico OCS ranks first with a mean estimate of 44.9 billion barrels. Alaska OCS is second with approximately 38.8 billion barrels.
- The United States is the third-largest producer of coal, with 27 percent of the world's total coal resources coming from the U.S.
- The natural resources that the United States can boast of include not only petroleum products, but uranium and nickel as well.
- The natural resources in America support the economy through the exporting of many of these resources. This creates millions of American jobs by way of manufacturing and production. The 94,000 mile coastline allows for shipping easily to other countries.
- The fertile soil allows for production of many different types of crops for the United States, with some of these crops being exported overseas.
- The timber industry is very strong in the Pacific Northwest, South Atlantic and the Gulf States.
- The Midwest has the opportunity to be the leader for cattle and corn. Livestock is also strong in the Southwest region of the States, making the U.S. the largest producer of beef.

It will not be easy replacing the dollar around the world. Right now, there are several countries where the U.S. dollar is the official currency for that nation. Some of these countries are Commonwealth of Puerto Rico, Ecuador, Republic of El Salvador, Republic of Zimbabwe, Guam, Virgin Islands, Democratic Republic of Timor-Leste, American Samoa, Commonwealth of the Northern Mariana Islands, Federated States of Micronesia (Six Sovereign Countries), Republic of Palau, and the Marshall Islands. In addition to these countries the British Virgin Islands and the British Turks and Caicos islands also use the U.S. dollar as their official currency of exchange. (*Source-Encyclopedia Britannica, Inc. Britannica Book of the Year 2015*)

The U.S. dollar is widely accepted and used for commerce in both Mexico and Canada. It's also accepted in many tourist destinations like the Commonwealth of the Bahamas, Barbados, Bermuda, the Cayman Islands, Saint Maarten, St Kitts and Nevis, the ABC Islands of Aruba, Bonaire, Curacao, and the BES Islands, just to name a few. In addition to this, several countries use the dollar along with their own currencies. I am not going to take the time to list all of them, but many countries have dual currencies in circulation. In addition to this, several countries use the dollar as a reserve in their central bank in order to back their currencies, and as we discussed earlier regarding the petrodollar most of the oil in the world is bought and sold in dollars. This is why nations trade using dollars. This is not just a matter of the dollar being used as a reserve by central banks. This is also a matter of nations and their citizens using the dollar around the globe for commerce and exchange.

All of these things add up to make the dollar stronger than most people realize. It is not just a reserve currency! It is a petrodollar. It is the official currency for several nations around the world. Out of the 13 trillion USD in circulation, about two thirds are beyond the borders of America and in use around the globe.

There are other aspects to this GCR conspiracy theory that make no sense. Some believe that the GCR is part of bible prophecy, so they accept it on that merit alone without researching anything else about the GCR theory. Some believe that an overnight dollar crash and a GCR event will be a prelude to the mark of the beast. Let me just say here and now that this conspiracy theory has absolutely nothing to do with bible prophecy. My personal research into the mark of the beast and other bible prophecy seems to indicate something very different.

Don't get me wrong. I'm not saying that the dollar will never be replaced as a reserve currency. I'm not saying that the dollar won't weaken over time. Nor am I saying that nations around the world will never use another currency. The truth is the dollar hasn't been the only currency used as a reserve in the past. It can be replaced over a period of time, although it will be a gradual transition.

What I am saying is this; there will not be an overnight crash that makes the dollar completely worthless around the world. It will not be shoved out of central banks overnight and be replaced with some new global super currency put together by the IMF. If and when the dollar is replaced it will be a gradual process. It will take time; probably years if not decades. It will not be an overnight event like some GCR promoters claim! There will not be an overnight crash of the U.S. dollar that will have an end result of making every gold, silver, dong, or dinar holder wealthy beyond their wildest dreams!

13 TRILLION U.S. DOLLARS ARE NOT GOING TO CRASH OVERNIGHT AND MAKE THE 40 TRILLION DINAR OUTSIDE OF THE BANK OF IRAQ WORTH 300,000 TIMES MORE IN VALUE!!!

Can you see the absurdity in this belief?

So let's do a brief review. Right now Iraq has 40 trillion dinar outside of the bank in Iraq. The exchange rate in 2009 was 1170 to the dollar. It moved four pips to 1166:1 in 2012, and was then devalued to 1182:1 in 2015. So as you can see, there has been a pretty steady exchange rate since 2009 with some slight fluctuations.

In 2009 Iraq had 21 trillion, 776 billion dinar outside of their banks. In 2014 Iraq had over 36 trillion outside of the banking structure. That means that in five years Iraq put an additional 14 to 15 trillion dinar into circulation outside of the banking structure! This is more than America's M2 money supply. Their population has not grown dramatically in this time period, so that couldn't have been the reason for the increase.

As I stated earlier two thirds of America's money supply is outside the border of the United States. Therefore, two thirds of America's money supply does not have a direct impact on inflation here in America because it is not used here. This leads me to ask two questions.

1. Why hasn't the dinar been consumed by hyperinflation?
2. How has their exchange rate remained so stable? After all, the dinar will revalue to fight inflation right? Why has there been virtually no movement of the exchange rate? Why have there been low single digit inflation rates in Iraq?

The answer to me is obvious. They have been exporting their currency. Based on what I consider a conservative calculation I suspect that there are slightly more than 30 trillion dinar outside of Iraq's borders today. If that is the case then this means that there are really only about 7 to 10 trillion dinar in circulation within Iraq's borders.

That's not bad for a currency that is only supposed to be used in Iraq! This is why hyperinflation has not collapsed the currency. This is why the exchange rate has been so stable. This is why their foreign currency reserves have been growing at a faster pace than normal. Here are Iraq's annual GDP growth figures according to Trading Economics:

2009 - 5.81 percent
2010 - 5.86 percent
2011 - 8.58 percent
2012 - 13.9 percent
2013 - 6.6 percent
2014 - 2.1 percent.

This is the same period that we are to believe that Iraq released 15 trillion dinar into their local economy.

If you are wondering why this does not make sense the answer is simple. Iraq is exporting their currency, and as their currency leaves the country it is exchanged for U.S. dollars. If over 30 trillion dinar left Iraq then that means that over $30 billion worth of other currencies (mostly USD) entered Iraq. This dinar investment/scam is bigger than most people realize. I think we would be surprised to see the real number of investors who purchased dinar. How many have bought this worthless paper due to a fictional GCR event?

This is massive and it is global! Every investor gave his or her dollars to Iraq in order to get dinar! In countries where the wages and cost of living are lower, the investment in the dinar is probably much smaller than in the US, UK, Canada, and Australia. I suspect that over ten million people from around the world have bought this currency with the hope of becoming wealthy when the RV finally comes. The prevailing belief is this event will take place when the GCR event kicks in. If and when Iraq does finally redenominate it will become big news. It will devastate millions of lives.

It's important at this point to note that Iraq has been dipping into their reserves. Much of their reserves came from oil sales and their economy, but about 20 to 25 percent came from exporting their currency. So even though their overall currency supply has dropped, the currency outside of the banking system has steadily increased.

Dinar gurus are pumping the global currency reset in an effort to provide a plausible justification for an unprecedented revaluation of Iraq's overprinted currency. They steal talking points from people that sell gold and silver in order to sell the dinar community on the idea that there is still hope for this worthless paper.

The Mechanics of an overnight dollar crash

Now that we see how entrenched the U.S. dollar is around the world today, hopefully you are beginning to see why an overnight crash as described by the GCR is impossible! It can't happen without completely destroying the global economy and its global governmental structure! This would be the equivalent of a nuclear holocaust or an invasion by space aliens wiping out mankind!

With little real evidence we are to believe that the world will end in one night as everyone around the world chooses to abandon the dollar, while at the same time the global population "discovers" that the dollar is a fiat currency. This is an extremely unlikely scenario because if everyone abandons the dollar they also choose to abandon the wealth that it represents. The global collection of T-bills becomes worthless in one night! Currencies around the world would collapse. That's why this conspiracy theory is responsible for turning many people into preppers.

When I read through conspiracy theory websites I see them describe how this is going to happen. Usually it starts with the collapse of the stock market followed by global hyperinflation. Countries around the world abandon the dollar. Those dollars make their way back to America and hyperinflation comes with it as those dollars enter the economy. All of this happens in one night, or it may take a few days for the entire effect to set in. The dollar crashes, and much of the world's wealth is gone or it is transferred into gold and silver.

Another scenario is that people around the world abandon the dollar that the evil Americans forced into central banks around the world. Then currencies all revalue based on natural resources that are at each nation's disposal. The dollar drops in value and other currencies rise as oil and other resources begin to back currencies. When the dollar makes its way back to America gold and silver will go up and hyperinflation will kick in because the central bank can't stop creating money. Inflation may be preceded by deflation, but in the end the dollar completely crashes through hyperinflation.

Both of these scenarios are wrong. Many people believe them, and as a result they buy gold, silver, foreign currencies, newsletters, prepper materials, guns, ammunition, bomb shelters, and several other products that will prepare them for the end of the world! At this point we need to stop and take a look at the real mechanics of this thing.

In order for a real overnight dollar crash to happen every nation that sells oil will need to stop selling oil in dollars overnight. Not only that, Arab nations have a lot of America's debt in the form of treasury bonds. When the dollar collapse happens those bonds become worthless. This action will wipe out the wealth in all of those oil producing nations. Also, as I mentioned there are 14 other countries that use the dollar as their official currency. These countries would need to stop using the dollar in one night and replace it with something else. In addition to all of this, I mentioned several countries like Bahamas, Barbados, Bermuda, and the Cayman Islands, that allow tourist to spend dollars, and they allow the dollar to circulate alongside of their own currency. That would need to end in one night. Then there are several more countries like Iraq that use the dollar along with their own currency to conduct regular business. That would also need to end in one night.

Besides all of this, almost every nation has dollars in their reserves to back their currency. Brazil, Russia, India, China, and South Africa have over 4 trillion U.S. dollars in their combined reserves. That money would need to leave their central banks in one night, and those nations would need to find another reserve to back their currency … OVERNIGHT! In addition to this, every nation that conducts trade using U.S. dollars would need to use some other currency to conduct trade, and they would need to abandon the use of the dollar ... OVERNIGHT!!

Also, the U.S. exports about on average about 1.86 trillion dollars of goods every year. All U.S. exports would need to stop using the U.S. dollar, and the U.S. would need to find and use some other currency for exports ... OVERNIGHT! Given the fact that raw materials are included in these exports and demand for these materials remain high, abandoning the total use of the dollar would be hard to accomplish. In addition to this all imports would need to stop because the dollar is no longer valid. As every nation around the world would no longer accept U.S. dollars, imports would dry up drastically driving up global unemployment. This would have a huge impact on China's economy as they no longer have the export demand to support their job base. Their entire economy will collapse!

At this point I have one obvious question; how is all of this supposed to happen in just one night? I can tell you it won't even happen in a week. In order to go through a dollar crash like the global currency reset people predict, everyone around the world would need to stop using the dollar all at the same time! This is a crazy belief to say the least.

Again, it's important to note that I'm not saying that the dollar can't be replaced. Its role in world commerce can be diminished, and over time the dollar can make its way out of central bank reserves. Another medium can be chosen for selling oil. Countries that don't have their own currency can find a different currency to be their official currency. But this won't happen overnight. It won't happen in a week or a month. It will take a gradual process. It may take years. This is assuming that there is another currency out there that can do what the dollar does, and we don't know of anything yet that can!

As you can see, a global overnight reset or a total dollar crash is akin to an end of the world event where everyone abandons the use of the dollar, while at the same time throwing away all the wealth that was acquired by using the dollar in the first place! It's not going to happen!

Chapter Ten - The Origins Of The Global Currency Reset

So where did this myth of the GCR come from? Well, a little digging around will show you that it came from something called NESARA. If you've never heard of NESARA you're not alone, but according to Wikipedia:

"NESARA is an acronym for the proposed National Economic Security and Reformation Act, a set of economic reforms suggested during the 1990s by Dr. Harvey Barnard. Barnard claimed that the proposals, which included replacing the income tax with a national sales tax, abolishing compound interest on secured loans, and returning to a bimetallic currency, would result in 0% inflation and a more stable economy. The proposals were never introduced before congress, and the only congressman known to have commented on the bill is Ron Paul, dismissively, and through a spokesman."

Many conspiracy theorists claim that NESARA was secretly signed into law by President Clinton in March of 2000. I checked the congressional record for the 1990s. Then I did a search through the entire database. This is what the search result said. *"NESARA does not occur in the database."* Then I did a search for National Economic Security And Reform Act. It was not in the congressional record at all. This means that this bill never came before congress.

This means that if NESARA never came before congress then it never became law!

However, NESARA has become a cult-like conspiracy theory promoted by Shaini Goodwin.

She claims the act was actually passed with additional provisions. She also claims George W. Bush and the Supreme Court have kept it hidden. In 2000 Barnard decided to release his proposal for NESARA on the internet. Soon after this, a person known as "Dove of Oneness" began posting about NESARA on internet forums.

Dove of Oneness has been identified as Shaini Goodwin. She was a former student of The Ramatha School of Enlightenment, founded by Judy Zebra Knight aka Judith Darlene Hampton. Knight teaches new age beliefs, and her teachings have attracted people like Shirley MacLaine and Linda Evans. Among the bizarre teachings is the belief that a convert to this teaching is god! Knight has appeared on U.S. TV shows such as Larry King and The Merv Griffin Show.

Goodwin has embellished and added to NESARA. She refers to "white knights", most of who are high-ranking military officials who have been struggling to have the NESARA law implemented despite opposition from George Bush. Barnard became aware of Goodwin's description of NESARA before his death in 2005. He denied that NESARA had been enacted into law or that it had even been assigned a tracking number, and he condemned Goodwin's assertions as a disinformation campaign. Since Goodwin began commenting on NESARA, other Internet-based conspiracy theorists have attached themselves to it, giving NESARA a life of its own.

NESARA will attach itself at times to legitimate economic issues to gain credibility. It can be found in the fair tax movement and it has shown up at Tea Party events, lurking at such functions while looking for converts. It has also attached itself to something called CMKX, and it talks about the payout of CMKX. Using terms like "global settlements" and referencing the White Knights. NESARA has attached itself to the RV of the Iraqi dinar as well. These White Nights are the men who will implement this supposedly secret law.

This opens up a completely new world as to why the dinar has not revalued yet! The terms "global currency reset" and "global settlements" first began with NESARA. According to current NESARA doctrine, when the dinar revalues the government will make the CMKX pay out. This will cause the White Knights to enforce the law, and the entire world resets, and then space aliens will show up on planet Earth and introduce themselves. I am not making this up! This is what they believe! They believe that we are being watched right now, and that as soon as all this stuff happens aliens will fly here in their spaceships.

Investigators who have researched Goodwin's claims found that she began commenting on NESARA in connection with Omega Trust, a fraudulent investment scheme whose creator Clyde Hood was on trial at the time. According to Goodwin, Omega Trust investors would receive their returns after NESARA was announced. Goodwin repeatedly predicted that the NESARA announcement would occur in the very near future, although in later years she was more reserved in these predictions.

The Omega Trust still lives on in the Internet world as a supposed global poverty relief program, and in part as a global currency reset. This is the origins of the global Currency reset belief.

The Coming Dollar Crash

As this thing evolved, opinions changed. Not everyone who believes in the GCR believes in the garbage that NESARA teaches. It is important to note that this does not represent every speculator. There is a smaller portion of people who actually believe the things that NESARA teaches. People pick and choose from different aspects of the GCR theory, and use different definitions in explaining it. I just felt that it was proper to cover the origins of the catch phrases "global currency reset" and "global settlements".

The dollar crash definition says that there is a coming collapse to the U.S. dollar. This is due in part to the United States debt, and in part to the overprinting of the U.S. dollar. People have been predicting the demise of the dollar for years. They will site the events that happened in 2008 as proof. Most of these people don't know or can't explain why the 2008 meltdown happened in the first place. This GCR crowd will rewrite history and make up quotes from the Founding Fathers in an effort to sound legitimate.

The basic belief here is that the dollar will lose reserve status around the world and it will become unstable. When this happens, countries around the world will replace or remove their reserves, and currencies like the dinar will revalue as a result. Gold and silver sellers have been predicting the end of the dollar for some time now, and the GCR event is used to exaggerate conditions, which leads to more gold and silver sales.

Dinar Gurus have taken this a step further and said that the collapse of the dollar and the GCR event will be the event that brings about a revalue in the Iraqi dinar. Therefore, it does not matter about the history of revalues because something is getting ready to happen that has never happened before in history. Then the claim is made that people cannot understand this new system and they cannot escape fiat currency terms. Sometimes the idea brought to dinar forums is that the dinar will use Iraq's resources to revalue its currency rather than the U.S. dollar.

A rabbit trail of this belief says that countries will give values to their currency based on the resources that a particular nation has. Certain commodities that are in that nation such as oil will determine the currency value. The IMF will force all nations to place a different value on their currency based on national resources.

Another belief is that the IMF will force all nations to simply revalue their currency. The dollar will go down because it is over printed and the dinar will go up. Gold and silver will go up as well. This belief is slightly different, as it has nothing to do with a nation's resources. This is popular among gold and silver sellers. Many of these precious metals gurus are currently spreading this hype, saying that value will transfer from the dollar to precious metals.

Another belief is that reserves around the world will be replaced with a group of currencies or a basket of currencies, thus replacing the dollar. While this is the only plausible aspect of the GCR theory and it has some merit, it will not happen overnight and it will not result in a total removal of the dollar or a revalue that will make every dinar holder wealthy.

Then there is another aspect of the GCR belief that claims it is a part of biblical prophecy. People subscribe to it because they believe it is a fulfillment of bible prophecy. To these people money mechanics don't matter because they take their faith in scripture and misapply it to the fictional GCR event.

When the reset event happens, everyone around the world will abandon the use of the dollar globally. All T-bills and American debt will be called in at once. Different currencies around the world will revalue as an entirely new monetary system is created, and all of those abandoned dollars will make their way back to America as nations no longer have central banking reserves to back their currency!

These are just some of the different definitions of GCR. As crazy as all this sounds, "GCR" proponents can't explain what they're trying to convey beyond throwing around a few buzzwords like "fiat currency" and "fractional reserve banking".

The people who push the fearmongering related to the GCR all have an agenda. They have something to sell, something to gain, and money to make from the fearmongering. Some gold and silver gurus and precious metal dealers push this as a tactic to get people to find a safe haven in precious metals. Some currency dealers push this GCR event and claim that it will cause all currencies to realign and the dollar will be worth a lot less and all foreign currencies will be worth a lot more. All of this pumping is an effort to get you to invest in over inflated currencies.

Gurus who exaggerate the dinar currency scam claim that when the GCR event happens the dinar will be worth a lot more and the dollar will be worth a lot less. This is how this mythical GCR event is used to increase sales. These pumpers only attribute the effects of over printing currency to America. According to them, other countries that overprint their currencies will be unscathed from the effects when the GCR event kicks in.

Some groups use the fictional GCR event to sell newsletters and memberships. Their intel is supposed to keep people informed of the impending doom. Most of the people who fall for this do not have a clue as to how the money mechanics associated with these terms really work. So let us explore it

Chapter Eleven - Problems Associated With a Reset

Many of these currency pumpers say that currencies will revalue based on a nation's gold supplies after the GCR event kicks in. They claim that the BRICS nations process and retain more gold then all the other countries combined. They talk about how much gold and silver China imports, and make the claim that China is now getting ready for the GCR event. The claim is China is adding all their imported gold to their currency reserves

This is another perfect example of an outrageously false claim. The BRICS have certainly been importing more gold and silver, but over half of what they import is consumed in industrial use and the demand for jewelry.

"In 2013, the country of China produced 342 tons of gold and consumed 840 tons thus importing 498 tons." That is not even remotely the same as the lie "China has been secretly adding 498 tons to their currency reserves every year!"

The same is true of India. They use nearly all of what they import on jewelry. That is why the Indian government slapped a 10% duty on gold bullion and a 15% import duty for gold jewelry. Most gold in Asia that is imported is going to private citizens, not central banks! Combined Eurozone gold reserves alone are more than the combined BRICS reserves! So that's even more propaganda that these GCR gurus have told.

Precious metals like silver are used in industry as well. I remember reading somewhere that one 42-inch flat screen TV has one ounce of silver in it. In addition to this, there's a lot of silver underground that is being mined, and a lot of this silver goes straight to industrial use. Check out the last chapter of this book and look at the top ten silver mines in the world today. These mines are making massive amounts of silver available to industry.

More gold has been going into China's central bank reserves, but it is only a small fraction of what they have been importing. By July of 2015 China had 1658.42 tonnes of gold for the purpose of currency backing. By July of 2016 China had 1823.3 tonnes of gold. So we see it is only a fraction of imported gold that goes to the reserves. In addition, China has been printing a lot more currency. Back in 2013 China had 120 trillion yuan in circulation. Today China has over 151 trillion yuan in circulation. For the last 10 years, their gold reserves have consistently represented 2 percent of their currency supply. As for *"revaluing all national currencies based on gold in a Global Reset",* here is gold's share in the national reserves by country:

76% USA
71% Portugal
70% Germany
69% Italy
65% France
63% Greece
63% Netherlands
45% Austria
38% Belgium
20% Spain
16% Russia
11% South Africa
09% UK
07% Iraq
06% India
02% Saudi Arabia
02% China

01% Brazil

Look at these links to verify the amounts you see above. The numbers are from the year 2016.
http://en.wikipedia.org/wiki/Gold_reserves#Officially_reported_gold_holdings
http://www.imf.org/external/np/sta/ir/IRProcessWeb/colist.aspx

Ninety-eight percent Of China and Brazil's wealth is through holding paper currency from other countries, including trillions of paper USDs. Ninety-three percent of Iraq's wealth is USD paper. Ninety-four percent of India's wealth is once again paper USDs. It really is time to drop the total mental delusion that:

- We are going back on a 100% full reserve gold standard. There simply is not enough gold in the world, which is why we left the gold standard in the first place! The entire combined GLOBAL reserves used to back currency are around 33,000 tonnes or around $2.5 Trillion worth. Compare that to the $80 trillion global economy and you soon see why this cannot happen.
- Going back on a gold standard will cause Iraq's economy and currency to soar and the USA to plummet because Iraq holds a tiny 89.8 tons of gold, which is less than the amount held by Romania or Libya!

If the U.S. dollar tanks and becomes worthless overnight, these BRICS nations will also lose all their wealth overnight! That's why GCR pumpers try to get around this by also claiming that when this event happens, national currency values will be backed by their natural resources.

Basing a currency's value on vague, unspecified resources simply lying in the ground is total nonsense. As for backing the dinar with oil, Iraq may have as much as 140 billion barrels of oil. At a price of $100 per barrel that is only equivalent to $14 trillion in assets.

HOWEVER, that $14 trillion worth of oil is going to be spread over the next 127 years in the form of 3.0 million barrels per day of actual production. If Iraq increases exports to 4 million barrels, then that $14 trillion worth of oil will still be spread over the next 96 years. As of this writing oil is about $42.07 dollars a barrel. The price of oil has been falling around the world as global production increases, so that $100.00 price is a best case scenario.

Some highly deluded people apparently think that 140 billion barrels will be magically teleported out of the ground after the mythical GCR event happens, and then all of that oil will be donated to the CBI. It will be stuck in some giant warehouse for backing the dinar tomorrow without a single drop being sold or used ever again! Others who see the problem with this scenario have bought into an idea floated by gurus that the dinars in the U.S. will be turned in to the U.S. Treasury where they will be used for oil credits for future purchases, overlooking the fact that the Treasury isn't in the oil business.

No country on this planet is going to squeeze every single year of economy from 2016-2142 AD into a 2016 currency's valuation! This is the absurd notion in a nutshell of the GCR event using resources to back currencies!

I could make the same ridiculous argument with the USA, and claim that the U.S. dollar is going to skyrocket if you count 127 years' worth of future U.S. exports which equals somewhere around $194 trillion or 13.8 times Iraq's worth in oil reserves.

Iraq has over 87.6 trillion dinar (M2) and 140 billion barrels of oil, or basically enough to back 607 dinar with 1 barrel worth $100. Nevertheless, that won't happen and oil will not back dinar because Iraq will consume around 1/5 to 1/4 of it themselves and export virtually all of the rest to other countries. In both cases, all that oil is no longer available to back the dinar!

The same thing applies with minerals. Let's say that a nation mines 1 million tons of aluminum resources. They use 300 thousand tons to build stuff and then they sell 700 thousand tons to other countries. How much do they have left for the function of currency backing? How much is left sitting in a pile doing absolutely nothing? **None!!!!**

Nations/companies pump oil and mine metals for two purposes: to use and to export. Once it is used or exported it is not available for backing anything. This is why simply quoting a nation's oil reserves and assigning an arbitrary GCR exchange rate to the currency based on that number is absurd.

It is also comically inconsistent. Apparently, Canada is going to fall and Iraq is going to rise due to Iraq's oil. This is hilarious given that Canada has 175 billion barrels of oil or 25% more oil than Iraq's 140 billion barrels. Canada has many other natural resources as well, and a diverse economy with a stable government. Why would they fall rather than Iraq? You simply can't base a nation's currency on the resources that nation has like GCR conspiracies claim.

If this were the case then China will also lose out bigtime due to being a net IMPORTER of virtually every raw resource going! They import everything from oil, LNG (liquefied natural gas), iron, copper, aluminum, titanium, uranium, coal, timber, rubber, etc. Why do people think China is running around Africa & South America buttering up the locals? Because they do not have enough resources to sustain what they consume, let alone any surplus left over to back 151 trillion yuan at some wonderful high rate! This is even more proof that the people shoveling this GCR belief have not even bothered to research any of the countries they are pumping!

Using non-recyclable resources like oil as currency backing and as an inflation hedge is also totally backwards and contradictory. As each year goes by, oil is used up or sold to someone else to use up. That oil is no longer available. Iraq cannot keep it in a vault for all eternity. They have to constantly sell it to fund the central government in place of taxes, or burn it internally for things like transportation, oil power stations, and construction. Iraq has to do this just out of necessity. It's their chief source of revenue.

Every time Iraq burns or exports a barrel of oil that oil will no longer be inside Iraq, backing the dinar. This action will make whatever GCR resource-backed currency peg more and more OVER-valued as each year goes by.

If Iraq has 140 billion barrels of oil and sells oil at the rate of 1.1 billion barrels per year and consumes more internally on top of that, then as each year goes by the resources backing its currency will increasingly dwindle, and they will need to LOWER the value of their currency peg vs oil. They will do this with an endless stream of annual DEVALUATIONS because if they lose currency-backing resources each year, then their resource-backed currency will lose value each year too!

In addition, their population is growing. They still have to print more money for liquidity purposes, amplifying this effect. What "genius" came up with this idea? Avoiding inflation by using a constantly dwindling resource that is naturally permanently inflationary is just stupid! If you want a hedge against inflation, you do not peg your currency to an asset that shrinks each year like oil, as that would have exactly the same long-term effect as printing too much fiat money and then not having the resources to back it!

There are just as many GCR gurus spewing out junk economics as there are gold and silver gurus and currency gurus. Many dinar investors cling to this GCR event because they are deathly afraid of admitting that Iraq is going to redenominate. This means they are left trying to find some alternative "magic millionaire elixir" to allow Iraq to keep 82 trillion dinar and somehow magically make it more valuable. They argue many GCR talking points to avoid admitting the blatantly obvious "elephant in the room"!

The Iraqi Dinar is 3,000 times weaker than the Kuwaiti Dinar simply because Iraq has printed 3,000 times more paper money than Kuwait. Either the people hanging around GCR conspiracy stuff are doomsday gold bugs predicting imminent $5,000 to $10,000 dollar gold prices every month since 1999, or they are dinar holders who have realized the absurdity of a 100,000% RV for Iraq. Yet strangely, they see nothing wrong in extending the same contorted logic to the whole planet to try to keep their pipedream going!

People keep talking about the oil that Iraq has as a means to base a new value on their currency. Countries do not base currency values on oil reserves and then once again on oil exports years later when the oil is actually drilled and sold. This is because you would be double counting everything, essentially trying to price in the exact same barrels of oil twice!

GCR propagandists tend to claim that the USA is losing its reserve status around the world. They claim that this will happen overnight when the GCR kicks in, but the USD's "reserve status" is not going to collapse to zero as if it was suddenly replaced by say the SDR (IMF Special Drawing Rights) which is expanded to include the BRICS countries as some GCR advocates are claiming. The USA's reserve status is not going to be replaced with a similar new supra-national reserve basket of currencies.

The USD is still going to make up a large chunk of that reserve simply out of economic necessity for trade! The USA still exports on average over $1.89 trillion in goods per year. This average per year is 3/4 of China's $2 trillion and the U.S. is still the #2 exporter out of some 190+ countries. Some people are wildly overreacting to a trend for more multinational reserves as somehow meaning a total collapse of the USA's economy. This is not true. Even in these dark times, exporting 3/4 of what China does with only 1/5th of the population (300 million people vs 1.5 billion people) is hardly something to be embarrassed about.

What will happen if countries stop selling oil in dollars? The consequences would be that their future inflationary risk will spread over a larger number of currencies. This means that they won't continue to devalue at the same rate with a peg to multiple currencies as they would with the USD only.

HOWEVER – that won't undo existing massive devaluation of the already inflated currencies like the dinar, dong, rupiah, yuan, rial, and others. They will remain weak until they redenominate simply because they have printed even more money in their own currencies than even the USA has printed. Abandoning the dollar if it becomes weak will simply hedge against further future devaluation, but it won't undo the past. Just like a cut in a budget deficit will slow the rate of increase of more future debt, but it will not shrink the existing debt.

The USA has printed $13 trillion dollars for 323 million Americans. This works out to around $42 thousand per American. Even if real figures are double that, it still works out to $84 thousand per American. That is a worst case scenario for counting 100% of all USD used only by Americans, this number includes the USD that is overseas.

However, Iraq has printed 87.6 trillion Dinar for 30 million Iraqi people. That works out to over 2.8 million dinar per Iraqi citizen! This is the classic scenario for past hyperinflation, when everyone in your country is a multi-millionaire in local currency units and yet the average annual salary is barely $5,000 in real international terms you see hyperinflation.

People who believe that a reduction in internationally held dollars will result in the dollar tanking and the yuan soaring need to get a grasp of how much money China has printed!

Which of the big nations have printed the most currency units?

1. China – 151 trillion yuan
2. Russia – 36.9 trillion rubles
3. India – 28.2 trillion rupee
4. USA – 13 trillion dollars
5. Eurozone – 10.5 trillion euros

Even if the USA's money supply was twice the official figures, it would still only be 1/5th the amount of China's supply.

Many people bash the Federal Reserve for creating too much money in order to bail out the banks, and rightly so. Strangely however, they seem to ignore the fact that China has printed ten times more yuan than the U.S. has printed dollars!

Inflation for all of the BRICS countries is actually higher than the USA's rate of 1.6%. Russia's is 6.1%, India's is 4.2%, China's is 2.1%, Brazil's is 7.8%, and South Africa's rate is 6.4% (based on Nov. 2016 numbers), assuming that everyone else is honest and the USA is the only country which underreports it! Food price inflation in China and India has been in double digits in many areas the past few years. Again, it is amazing how some people act like only the USA experiences inflation.

In short, Iraq moving away from a pure dollar peg may slow down the rate of future devaluation based on the Federal Reserve increasing the money supply, but what it WON'T do is cause the dinar's value to shoot up! This is because Iraq will continue to have well over 87.6 trillion dinar in circulation until they redenominate. It does not matter what the Federal Reserve does, as Iraq's problem is too many DINARS, not too many dollars!

It is a common guru fallacy that the dinar must be weak purely because of the dollar, which will be corrected by a mythical GCR event. This is nonsense. The dinar is also weak vs the Euro (1590:1), GBP (1919:1), Gold (1.475m dinar / oz), and Silver (23,157 Dinar / oz), commodities (eg, Wheat ($272/mt) is 317,457 Dinar / mt (metric tonne), etc.

The dinar is weak because Iraq has printed too many dinars. No matter what the dollar does, the dinar will continue to be weak until they reduce their 87 trillion dinar money supply back down to the 87 billion it used to be before the hyperinflation of the 1980s and 1990s. The only way to reduce it that much is through a redenomination. The USD could vanish off the face of the earth overnight, and the dinar would still have a rate of 1238:1 vs the Euro!

The same is true of the dong – it's utterly mind-boggling how some people can sit there with a straight face and say that the GCR event will adjust the undervalued dong, when the dong's 22748:1 rate vs the dollar is a direct result of the Vietnamese Central Bank printing a jaw dropping 5.5 QUADRILLION+ dong! For clarity's sake, that is 5,519 trillion dong vs the Federal Reserve's 13 trillion dollars!

There is some truth to the move to a multipolar financial reserve world, but there's also a whole lot of hysterical guru propaganda surrounding an increase in value for the dinar/dong by more than 100,000%, via either RV or some mythical GCR event.

By the way, the move away from the dollar's international reserve status to a mix of dollars, euros, yuan, etc., is more about ending a downward spiral of future unilateral Federal Reserve devaluations, or the usual U.S. vs China power-bloc politics than it is some 100,000%+ return get-rich-quick scheme that involves convincing amateur speculators that the most inflated currencies on Earth are just unfairly undervalued rather than inflated! This is about 99 percent of all dinar/dong RV pumping in a nutshell!

The same holds true for gold and silver. We are supposed to believe that due to an overprinted dollar, gold and silver will magically shoot up after this GCR event. Are we to believe that right now gold and silver remain greatly suppressed so that the dollar can retain the value it has, and all precious metals are undervalued? As some gold sellers put it, *"a transfer of wealth will happen from paper to real money after the GCR event takes place."* In this case, their claim seems to be that precious metals are the real money and all paper is fiat currency backed by nothing. The GCR event will realign everything. That is gold and silver pumping in a nutshell!

Iraq has over 71 trillion dinar in their M1 alone. That entire dinar supply is meant to be used by a population of 32 million people. According to the dinar currency laws, the dinar is only supposed to be in circulation inside of Iraq. It is not to be used outside of Iraq for exchange and it has no value outside of Iraq.

America has 13 Trillion U.S. dollars in their M2 for a population of over 300 million people. About two thirds of the U.S. dollar is exported outside of America's borders. It is used around the world in currency reserves and by other nations as a means for exchange. As we can clearly see, there are not enough dollars in existence to support any kind of revalue for the amount of dinar outside of the banking structure.

Chapter Twelve - Don't Believe the Hype

"The wisdom of the prudent is to give thought to their ways, but the folly of fools is deception." (Proverbs 14:8 NIV)

In the last few chapters, we talked about the problems with the GCR. We talked about and exposed NESARA for the conspiracy theory that is. We dealt with some of the many definitions to the term "global currency reset". The last chapter was getting somewhat long, so I decided to stop at a certain point and continue in this chapter with more information. I'll be jumping in the middle of a thought process using a lot of information already covered in the previous chapter. So let's continue.

China

The IMF plays a major role in one of the definitions of the GCR. According to past lies by certain metals pumpers, the IMF was going to force all nations to revalue their currency by the end of March 2014 and the new values of these currencies would be based on other things. The dollar would have been worth a lot less because of this event.

Not only is this absurd, it is not even practical. As I said before, people only attribute the effects of overprinting currency to America. They ignore the effects it has on all other nations that do the same thing. They act as if America is the only one that is going to suffer for this practice and all other nations are immune.

While it is true that America has 13 trillion dollars, China has printed over 151 trillion yuan! That is 10 times the amount of America's dollar. People are overreacting to the events of October 1st, 2016 when China's currency became part of the international basket of currencies. Many in the GCR crowd are now predicting that China's currency will replace the dollar. These people seem to overlook the fact that China has well over 3 trillion U.S. dollars in their currency reserves to back their currency. They also seem to forget that China's currency is pegged! Most currencies that are used for currency backing float. China is still not willing to give up that element of control. They want reserve currency status for a pegged currency!

There was an IMF report that said the yuan's real exchange rate is undervalued by 5%-10%. China does this because their economy depends on exports. If they raise their currency's value because of a GCR event or because the IMF orders them to do it, that would make their products more expensive. That would in turn lead to a decrease in exports! By the way, this applies to all of the other BRICS nations as well. In fact, it would apply to every other country period! You are not going to get every country to comply with currency rates imposed by the International Monetary Fund. This is absurd! There would always be some defectors, and that would cause everyone to ignore arbitrary IMF-imposed GCR rates. That's because if America's currency drops in value while at the same time other currencies rise in value, then nations like China will lose their export advantage!

In the past China has always sought to maintain an undervalued currency, which in effect acted as a 30 to 40 cent tariff on all goods coming into their country. That allowed their exports to increase, and at the same time allowed them to control imports. Countries with overprinted and inflated currencies have a greater chance to export more goods because their currency values are low, which translates to a strong manufacturing economy if their manufacturing base is developed. That's why they print their currencies into oblivion!

These nations are not going to surrender the sovereignty of their currency value to the IMF. The IMF will not be able to force China to raise its currency's value, especially based on some fictitious GCR event. In order for that to work, the IMF would need to control the printing demands for every nation. All those countries would need to do to lower their currency's value once again is to print even more currency behind closed doors. Is the IMF going to tell each nation how much currency they can print? This notion is ridiculous to say the least.

As far as revaluations go, China serves as a great example. Over the past decade, China revalued the yuan by a total of about 35% vs. the dollar. This was spread out across multiple steps. This is what real life RVs look like; a couple of percentage points here and few more there a few years later.

Even today, with China's deliberate under-pegging aberration, you are still only talking about a 5-10 percent undervaluation. About 15 percent is the absolute highest estimate, which is nothing even remotely close to a 100,000% revaluation!

The gurus' pumping of the dinar by trying to pretend that the dinar must return to a 1980s exchange rate while ignoring the fact that its money supply is now 4,000 times higher than what it had been in the 1980s is ludicrous. This is the prime reason its rate fell in the first place!

However, as long as China is a net exporter of goods they simply won't want a massively stronger currency. In fact, it will hurt Chinese businesses by making everything relatively more expensive for non-Chinese to import goods from China in all future trade. Having a stronger currency is no good if it kills off export growth!

It is also true that China has cancer villages and many other environmental issues to overcome due to lax environmental controls. It remains to be seen what kind of toll that will take on their economy.

That's why so many nations are miffed at the Fed for QE, because they believe that this action will lower the value of the USD and this will affect the exports from other nations.

Imagine what would happen to America's economy if the U.S. dollar suddenly dropped significantly due to hyperinflation. The amount of imports would suddenly decrease as their prices would soar. Now how would it affect China if all currencies were suddenly reset and China no longer had its edge, and the U.S. had a significantly lower value attached to its currency?

U.S. interest rates have been practically nil since the economic crisis began back in 2008. Gold and silver will react negatively to the news of a possible imminent increase in interest rates, because any increase in interest rates will strengthen the dollar.

QE was also an effort to boost the economy. As we have seen, the unemployment rates dropped and the U.S. economy finally began a small recover. As I expect, the Federal Reserve eased up on QE and the dollar has strengthen as a result. Q.E. officially ended in 2014 and it was the best year for the dollar since 2005. When this happened it had a negative effect on the prices of gold and silver, but the people who sell precious metals and push this GCR will not point this out.

Iraq

Here is Iraq's current money supply.

Iraqi dinar outside of the banks in circulation = 40 trillion
Iraq M0 = 60.818 trillion
Iraq M1 = 70.756 trillion
Iraq M2 = 87.572 trillion

The reason dinar gurus won't repost this or even talk about it is pretty obvious. Iraq still has over 40 Trillion in physical banknotes alone, and there's a total of only 10 trillion between their M0 and M1 due to the primitive nature of Iraq's banking system.

Their money supply is so bloated that there is no possible way for them to revalue to even a penny! No GCR event can overlook this. If there was a GCR event and the IMF raised the value of the dinar as people claimed, then it would not be long until hyperinflation would collapse the currency entirely due to the amount in circulation!

Religious Point of View

There are those who present the GCR as part of biblical prophecy. It is believed that this event will move everyone closer to the mark of the beast, a one-world economy, and the rule of the Antichrist. Christians who know little about biblical prophecy have fallen for this, and that's the main reason many of them invested in the dinar in the first place. Who can argue with bible prophecy?

The fact is, this mythical GCR has nothing to do with bible prophecy. That's nothing more than false doctrine. Some people have just placed their faith in junk economics rather than what is actually taught in bible prophecy. I have studied the Bible for many years, and I love to research the subject of prophecy. The mark of the beast is totally different from anything related to a global currency reset, and it is issued during the time of the Antichrist by the false prophet. Even though many dinar gurus are false prophets, they're not the ones the Bible is talking about.

Buzz Words

Most people cannot really explain the mechanics of a GCR beyond using buzz words like "global reset", "fiat currency", "fractional reserve banking", and "linear thinking". These are just some of the buzz words that I have seen on currency-related websites. Let me provide some definitions to what these buzz words actually mean.

Fiat Currency

"Fiat" is the Latin word for "it shall be". Most currencies that we have used in America were based on physical commodities like as gold or silver at one time, but fiat money is based solely on government decree. Fiat currency is money that a government has declared to be legal tender. Fiat currency isn't backed by any physical commodity, and thus can't be exchanged for such a commodity because it has no intrinsic value. The value of fiat money is derived from the relationship between supply and demand rather than the value of the material that the money is made of or the commodity it represents.

Some people consider the U.S. dollar a fiat currency because they believe that it is backed by nothing. The Iraqi dinar is not considered a fiat currency by these same people because it has reserves backing it. Incredibly, the fact is 93 percent of what backs the dinar is the so-called fiat **U.S. DOLLAR**! And this gives the dinar value ..... how? How will the GCR regulate a currency that gets its value from the U.S. dollar if that dollar crashes overnight? If the dollar falls then the dinar falls too! So do the yuan and many other currencies around the world. The dollar will not fall while every inflated currency backed by the dollar rises! This is absurd!

The U.S. Congress has designated that Federal Reserve Banks must hold collateral equal in value to the Federal Reserve notes in circulation. This collateral is held primarily in the form of U.S. Treasury, federal agency, and government-sponsored enterprise securities.

This is how gold breaks down. There are 171,000 tons of gold above ground in the world today. 18 percent of that (or 32,000 tons) is held by central banks as reserves. Out of that the U.S. has 8,133.5 tons of gold, which makes up about 76 percent of the reserves held by the U.S.

The Federal Reserve Bank of New York holds 540,000 Gold bars alone. That is not bad for a fiat currency backed by nothing! Now compare that to the dinar that has a grand total of just 7 percent gold in their reserves. The rest of their reserves are U.S. dollars!

Now it's true, you can't exchange U.S. currency for the assets that back it. That is why it is considered a fiat currency; it is money by government law or decree. So what good is the currency if you can't exchange it for the assets that are used to back it? Well, the truth is there are assets that back the U.S. currency today, but it is still considered to be "fiat" because there is no exchange process regarding the assets the currency represents. It is still used to determine value in purchases around the world, and it us used to promote commerce by United States law.

Linear Thinking

If you are accused of "linear thinking" that means you can't understand the Global Currency Reset because you're just not able to think creatively. What that really means is that you pay too much attention to insignificant things like printed currency supplies and reserve-backed currencies, and that prevents you from seeing the truth. You pay too much attention to global economics, and you don't see the gold and silver opportunities that are based more on how money actually worked in the past. You need rose-colored 3D glasses.

Apparently, if you are not a linear thinker then you know that currency supplies don't matter, and nations can have as much of it as they want. It won't make any difference. Only the U.S. will be penalized for having too much currency because they are evil and bad. Every other country is good and as pure as the driven snow!

If you can't see that then you are a "linear thinker."

What a crock!!! Currency supplies do matter, and too much currency destroys the value - end of story! This applies not only to the United States, but to every nation around the globe. Perhaps that's the reason there have been over 70 redenominations over the past fifty years or so! This "linear thinking" line is just a catch phrase designed to shame you into believing all of the fearmongering that these idiots are trying to shovel!

Fractional Reserve Banking

As we discussed earlier, "fractional reserve banking" (or "FRB") is a process that expands the money supply. It has been said on some GCR sites that central banks will use this process to pay out new currency values after the GCR. The only problem with this is the fact that FRB is a process that is only used by the public banking system. Private central banks don't use it.

Consider this; FRB is a process that expands the money supply by monetizing the debt. In other words, when people participate in the loan process the debt amount becomes monetized. New money is created from debt, thus expanding the currency supply. Central banks don't do this; public banks do. Neither the Central Bank of Iraq nor any other central bank are going to go into debt using a method of debt monetization so that they can pay out a new value that was arbitrarily assigned to their currency by the IMF! That shows you how clueless some of these gurus are about economics!

The IMF

Christine Lagarde is the managing director of the International Monetary Fund. Some versions of the GCR theory name her as the one responsible for the upcoming GCR event. These gurus shoveling junk economics quote her Twitter page and watch her for clues.

Lagarde's exact tweet: *"We need a reset in the way the economy grows around the world"*. These precious metals dealers and dinar/dong gurus have somehow morphed this into *"All currencies are going to reset."*

All she was really talking about was resetting economies. The goal here is to boost economic growth to pre-2007 levels! BEFORE THE 2008 MELTDOWN! These factors include reducing unemployment and the rate of inflation. There is some banking reform through Basel III, which is really all about increasing balance sheets for banks. It has absolutely nothing to do with currency values! It is NOT a GCR guru-style statement of "let's pretend the world's most inflated currencies are not really inflated, and assign them all wonderful new higher values!"

People are just twisting the whole thing wildly out of context to mean overnight revalues of currencies and the demise of the dollar! All that most of these people are really doing is confusing the word economy with the word "currency". They are not interchangeable. It is possible to have a strong currency and weak economy. Greece, Portugal, and Fiji serve as examples. It is also possible to have a weak currency and a strong economy. South Korea, China, and Japan serve as examples of that.

A while back, the BBC released an article about the dinar. They actually quoted me in that article. They also quoted the IMF. The BBC claimed that according to the IMF the Dinar investment was fraudulent. By the way, this was a direct quote from the IMF.

The Truth Is

What do people mean when they say "global currency reset"? This in itself is a buzz phrase thrown around as though it has some sort of validity. The truth is it can be a complicated subject. Part of the reason for this is because there are so many different meanings attached to it.

The United States dollar is the most widely held currency in the allocated reserves today. A report released by the United Nations Conference on Trade and Development in 2010 called for abandoning the U.S. dollar as the single major reserve currency. Some have proposed the use of the International Monetary Fund's (IMF) special drawing rights (SDRs) as a reserve. As I said before, there is some truth to the move to a multi-polar financial reserve world, but many people are wildly overreacting to a trend for more multinational reserves as somehow meaning a total collapse of the U.S. economy and a revaluation of the worlds most inflated currencies.

The Global Currency Reset does not mean that the entire U.S. economy will collapse and the dollar will become worthless while the overprinted dinar, dong, and others become the new standard! That to me is the most absurd definition of the GCR out there!

Chapter Thirteen - The Final Analysis

Congratulations! If you got this far in the book you now know more about economics than 90 percent of the American people. You know more details about the lies propagated through gold and silver merchants, too. You know why we have had a surge in preppers, and you know more about currency scams than most people even want to know. Most people don't want to take the time to consider the points presented throughout this book. This is because economics can be very boring. Our school system has dumbed down our young people. Economic history should be taught in high school.

Today people spend money and they don't really think about what money is. They only think about what money does. Money has a past, and it has evolved over the years. In fact, money is still evolving. Money used to be gold and silver that had to be weighed on a scale. From there money became coins made from these metals. We saw the rise of fiat money in 1100 A.D. The paper currency used in Europe and America use to be a paper receipt that people got from the goldsmith in the 18th century. When people stored their gold in the goldsmith's shop, they were given a receipt. People began trading those paper receipts because it was easier than going down to the goldsmith's shop every time they wanted to retrieve their gold or silver to do an exchange. We also saw the rise of central banking systems during the 18th century. The paper receipts from gold became known as currency. It was the next step in the evolutionary process.

Over time, we left the gold standard. Our money system continued to evolve. Gold and silver was now an asset. Paper receipts became currency, and then currency became money. Before the Federal Reserve, our currency required precious metals like gold and silver to back it. These metals played an integral role in our financial policy. After the Federal Reserve, we slowly migrated from a monetary system where the dollar went from a gold based reserve system to a system where most of our money is expanded using debt. Debt is now turned into money. All of this happened at the same period of time when a massive global economy emerged.

Today, debt is monetized by a fractional reserve banking system. Gold is still in use as an asset, and it is kept in reserves. It is used as an asset to back almost every major currency around the globe. Only a percentage of currency is backed by this metal today. Many countries that have gold to back their currency will not allow you to exchange their currency for gold. The United States even has a gold reserve. However, not all currency around the globe has gold to back it. In fact, the lion's share of currency around the world is back by paper assets. Currencies are backed by other currencies that are monetized through a system of debt. Like it or not, that is what today's global system has evolved into. Money not only determines value, but it also represents labor in the form of debt.

I know that this sounds completely crazy, but consider this. Money = debt and debt = labor. Labor pays the debt that is monetized. That is how the system stays in balance, and that is how it works in today's society. Labor brings you money, which pays debt, and most money is monetized debt. This is the current system, and it has evolved to this strange condition over a long period of time.

Some modern government philosophies have it all wrong. Wealth is not generated through redistribution. True wealth is generated through labor and created over time. If a farmer looks at his field and does nothing there is no new wealth generated. If he plants and prepares for a harvest, then his labor will increase his wealth. This labor is monetized in the form of debt.

Some have said that labor is another word for slavery. "Debt equals slavery" as the claim goes. In regards to today's system I disagree. The difference is that with labor you have a choice. With slavery, you do not have a choice. Nobody is putting a gun to your head and telling you to get a job, buy a house, get a car, and get married and start a family. People do those things because they choose to. The money to pay for all those things comes from your labor, which you choose to use in order to pay the debts acquired by those things.

Some people may argue that the government debt is too large, and we are on the hook for that debt. We as American citizens are responsible for it. Labor will be the way to pay it back, and therefore it is slavery.

I think we are splitting hairs here. My only real point is that your personal debt is your choice. How you spend the money you earn is entirely up to you. That money you spend represents your labor, but at the same time it represents debt. Any debt you acquire represents future labor.

Money is still evolving. The checkbook is becoming history. Digital currency is on the rise, and paper currency is going away. We are headed for a cashless society as Americans carry less than $50 cash on average. We have credit cards and debit cards with computer chips in them. Transactions are even being done on our cell phones and over the internet. This whole monetary system is still changing and evolving in this modern digital age, and it will look completely different 50 or 60 years from now.

    This system is absolutely crazy to say the least, but the truth is our new global economy is too big to go back to the classic gold standard. There is not enough gold in the world to do this, and doing so would bring much more poverty to many nations around the world today. This is the main reason gold and silver merchants are predicting a 5,000 to 10,000 dollar price per ounce of gold! They are trying to fit the modern 80 to 100 trillion dollar economy into the classic gold standard era!

    Most of these gold and silver merchants don't remember all the problems that we had under the classic gold era. They don't know the reasons we left it. Let's do a quick review. Money could not be expanded and contracted as the national needs changed. There was not enough gold to go around during contraction laws regarding the greenbacks. That created more poverty. The money supply via gold and silver did not keep up with population growth. Currency supplies were being contracted while we were heading into the 1920s.

    The decline caused the unemployment rate to rise from 4% to nearly 12% by 1921! This was in large part due to the fact that banks were trying to conserve their gold reserves. The truth is, money backed by gold constantly led to crisis because most banks were worrying more about the gold they had in their possession than they were about currency expansion. During the 1920s there was an average of 70 banks failing each year. Prior to the Federal Reserve System, the average lifespan of a bank was merely five years. That is why Woodrow Wilson campaigned on banking reform! That is also why the Federal Reserve Act was debated in Congress for over four months. It's also why Senator Nelson Aldridge toured Europe studying central banking models, and why the Federal Reserve decisions are independent from congress, the senate and the president!

Even though there are hiccups in this crazy modern money system from time to time, this global economy is not going to totally crash overnight. It is actually much more stable than having an economy that uses the gold standard!

Think of all the things that happened in the last 25 years - the dotcom bubble, 9/11, wars in Iraq and Afghanistan, the 2008 meltdown, TARP, currency wars, and finally QE. All these things could not put an end to the current global system, but I submit to you that they would bring an end to any currency system backed by gold. This is why we left that system in the first place.

It is a proven fact that the economies that left the gold standard after the great depression were some of the first economies to recover. If today's system were to actually collapse, it would be felt around the world. No currency would be safe. Every country and every currency would feel the effect because in today's system all currencies are fiat. All values are perceived and they are all based on debt. All currencies are interconnected through the dollar.

The BRICS nations mainly use dollars to back their currency. At one point there were over 4 trillion dollars combined that were used to back their currencies. A total overnight crash of the dollar would devastate Brazil, Russia, India, China, and South Africa. It would also devastate

Iraq and the many other nations around the world that use the dollar as their main reserve. In the event of a global dollar crash, almost every country's currency would become worthless, and imports in the United States would come to a grinding halt.

Nations want low currency values, but more than that they need trading partners. If you remove the United States from the equation it would really have a devastating impact on China. As much as these nations scream because our dollar weakened after 2008, they also really understand that they cannot totally bankrupt their trading partners.

We have learned a great deal in this book; probably more about economics then we care to know. Once we get the facts straight, the truth sets us free. We are no longer driven by every wind of doctrine, being victims of fear and anxious for everything. What have we learned?

The United States dollar is not a fiat currency in the truest sense of the word. (Fiat = backed by nothing) The Federal Reserve does have some gold. In addition, the dollar is also backed with U.S. Treasury, federal agency, and government-sponsored enterprise securities.

We have also learned that while our dollar is printed in high quantities and the supply is huge, China has ten times the amount of currency we have. Their economy has grown to an incredible size! Their weak currency had little effect on their strong economy. Their reflex is to weaken their currency if their economy gets worse. I know that sounds backwards, but that is how they recover. In addition, many nations have a lot more of their currency printed than America does, yet America is portrayed as the only one who will suffer the consequences from overprinting.

In addition to this, we have also learned that while we have printed many dollars, about two thirds of our dollar supply remains exported. It is used by other nations as a reserve, and it is the only currency used by some nations as a means for exchange. It's used to buy and sell oil. Nations conduct trade with the dollar, and some nations use it as a second currency. This act keeps their currency strong, and holds inflation in check. The dollars that remain overseas do not have a direct impact on inflation here in the states.

I hope that you can understand by now that the dollar is really much stronger than what certain people are saying. The dollar is so entrenched that it will be impossible to get rid of it overnight. There is no overnight dollar crash coming that will devastate the global economy. In my opinion, the dollar happens to be one of the strongest currencies out there. For now, it remains the best option.

This does not mean that the dollar will not be replaced. It just means that it will take a lot of time to do this. It will be gradual and slow if it happens at all. We also need this international basket of currencies to contain U.S. dollars just out of a need for trade. The United States exports were $2.35 trillion in 2015. You need dollars to buy our exports! This is why the dollar will remain in the basket of currencies! The dollar will not suddenly be worth nothing.

This analysis does not mean that I approve of the Federal Reserve or its policies. It does not mean that I approve of the bank bailouts or TARP. All I am saying is that these policies are being misrepresented in global conspiracy circles. An overnight collapse of the dollar is not possible without an overnight collapse of the entire global monetary system. I believe that a sudden crash is highly unlikely. Fear mongering is being used to sell all kinds of products due to these conspiracy theories. Everyone has an agenda!

The truth is after the 2008 meltdown somewhere around 11 trillion dollars in wealth vanished as debt was erased from the books. This is the expanded money supply that was created from debt. Because global demand for the dollar remained strong that money needed to be replaced. Q.E. was a program that expanded the base money supply to make up for what was lost in the expanded money supply. For decades economists will be arguing over the outcome of this controversial program.

The Sales Pitch

There is a sales pitch used to sell certain types of products. Fearmongering dominates this sales pitch. I see many of these pitches on internet commercials, and I hear many commercials on talk radio. I also see a few of these types of commercials on television. They all seem to have the same type of approach and sales pitch.

They usually start by saying something like *"We predicted the 2008 meltdown"* or they may add, *"We warned about the housing bubble in 2008, and the dotcom bubble".* These statements are designed to make you think these people represented in the advertisement are financial experts. The statements may claim that the advertiser has successfully navigated through a series of bad economic events and brought wealth to many people.

The next statement is typically something like this. *"The Federal Reserve is printing too much money."* Which is followed by, *"A collapse of the dollar is coming!"* Sometimes this can be followed by *"this collapse will make the Great Depression look like a recession."* Sometimes this statement will follow *"How will you prepare for this financial collapse"* or *"how prepared are you for the collapse of the dollar?!"*

Ok, are you getting scared yet? That is what these statements are designed to do. These are just a few of the general statements that some of these commercials use.

Now the sales pitch begins. *"Not only can you avoid the pitfalls of the coming economic collapse, but you can actually profit from it!"* From here the product is pitched. Sometimes they offer you a free guide. This is so they can get your mailing address or email address. Then once they have those things you are bombarded with even more propaganda.

The people who do this all have an agenda. They all have something to sell. Sometimes they are selling gold and silver. Other times they are selling newsletters with investment advice, or maybe they have some books they want you to buy.

Sometimes these people will claim to have contacts and be on the inside of some government agencies or organizations. They may claim to have certain knowledge in an area of finance and present a successful background of some sort. All of this is in their résumé, which is in the advertisement.

I refer to these people as gurus because they give the illusion of being all knowing about their field through their résumé. They claim to have many contacts. There are currency gurus, there are economic gurus, and there are gold and silver gurus. A lot of the stuff these people shovel makes no sense to someone who has an actual economics education. After all, if the dollar is becoming so worthless, why are they seeking your dollars to fill their pockets?

The problem is the average American knows nothing about economics, and they do not want to know anything about economics. These gurus exploit that weakness and use fearmongering to target the uninformed. Then once you are good and scared they try to sell pointless, useless products that do nothing. The only thing they accomplish is to relieve the fear that they placed upon you in the first place. I find this highly unethical.

Don't get me wrong! There is nothing wrong with investing in gold or silver. In fact, I have invested in precious metals myself. I still have those investments today. But if you are buying these metals because you believe that the global economy is going to crash overnight and gold and silver will be the only thing left after the dust clears, then you are buying these items for the wrong reasons. Don't overleverage yourself!

Step back, take a deep breath, and use some common sense. Don't fall for the hype! Don't buy gold out of fear for your financial future. Invest in gold if you believe it has potential. Do real research, and don't fall for the GCR hype. Don't buy gold simply because you believe there is another financial meltdown coming and you will lose everything unless you buy some. That's all I'm saying. Buy gold for the right reasons.

Selling the idea that the world is going to end, and that you need to buy gold to avoid the destruction is how these guys make money. The same thing holds true for newsletters, books, food supplies, and foreign currency. You are not going to make any money buying a totally debased, overprinted currency that will one day magically revalue due to a fictional global currency reset. That is a pipedream that many gurus sell. If you have any of this currency your best bet is to sell it and get out now, even if you take a loss. It is better to lose a little money than to lose everything you have invested.

In the final analysis, fearmongering is utilized to exaggerate and sell you things you do not need. If something or someone has made fearmongering statements just remember this. Everyone has an agenda, and everyone is selling something. Question the motives of these salesmen. Question their résumé before you buy into the hype. These gurus don't know as much as they lead you to believe, and they're preying upon people who know nothing at all about economics.

It is ok to prepare for emergencies and to prepare for unseen events, but a coming overnight crash of the dollar is a bit absurd. In fact, it is wise to have emergency provisions and to stock up on food in case of emergencies.

Once again, I am not saying that the dollar will never be replaced, all I am saying is that it won't happen overnight and it will take a lot of time to do it because the dollar is deeply entrenched around the globe. The dollar will not become absolutely worthless as some claim!

Be careful of wolves in sheep clothing. Be careful of people who pretend to be Christian in order to gain your trust. Don't automatically trust someone just because they have a fish on their business card. Now you are no longer a victim. Steer away from these people. Remember the basic economics that this book contains and you will be all right. I will leave you with a few Bible scriptures about money. All of these quotes are from the HCSB version.

Leviticus 19:13 you must not oppress your neighbor or rob him. The wages due a hired hand must not remain with you until morning.

Proverbs 12:11 The one who works his land will have plenty of food, but whoever chases fantasies lacks sense. 12The wicked desire what evil men have, but the root of the righteous produces fruit.

Proverbs 13:11Wealth obtained by fraud will dwindle, but whoever earns it through labor will multiply it.

Proverbs 16:8 Better a little with righteousness, than great income with injustice.

Proverbs 22:16 Oppressing the poor to enrich oneself, and giving to the rich — both lead only to poverty.

Proverbs 28:20 A faithful man will have many blessings, but one in a hurry to get rich will not go unpunished. 21It is not good to show partiality —yet a man may sin for a piece of bread. 22A greedy man is in a hurry for wealth; he doesn't know that poverty will come to him.

Proverbs 28:25 A greedy person provokes conflict, but whoever trusts in the Lord will prosper.

Ecclesiastes 5:8 If you see oppression of the poor and perversion of justice and righteousness in the province, don't be astonished at the situation, because one official protects another official, and higher officials protect them.

Ecclesiastes 5:10 The one who loves money is never satisfied with money, and whoever loves wealth is never satisfied with income. This too is futile. 11When good things increase, the ones who consume them multiply; what, then, is the profit to the owner, except to gaze at them with his eyes? 12The sleep of the worker is sweet, whether he eats little or much, but the abundance of the rich permits him no sleep. 13There is a sickening tragedy I have seen under the sun: wealth kept by its owner to his harm. 14That wealth was lost in a bad venture, so when he fathered a son, he was empty-handed.

1Timothy 6:9But those who want to be rich fall into temptation, a trap, and many foolish and harmful desires, which plunge people into ruin and destruction. 10For the love of money is a root of all kinds of evil, and by craving it, some have wandered away from the faith and pierced themselves with many pains.

2 Timothy 1:7 For God has not given us a spirit of fear, but of power and of love and of a sound mind.

Chapter Fourteen - Trust But Verify

This book contains a lot of my opinions about money, but it also contains some indisputable facts from which I base my opinions. Everything that I talk about in the book can be found on the Internet. After all, that is where I got the information to begin with. Just by using Google, Yahoo, or Bing you can verify the numbers and the facts that are in this book. Everything I talk about is public information, and it is easily verified. This information is not a collection of government secrets from conspiracy theory websites.

The following is a list of resources and references that that are included in the eBook version of this book. These resources and references will allow the reader to narrow their search and continue their personal research. I would simply ask that you don't take my word for all the things you just read. Verify it with your own research. These are just some of the sites that provided the information used to write this book. There were many more sites that I found to verify the material I covered. There are over 90 links that should get you pointed in the right direction.

Trading Economics is a fantastic economic website. You can find a lot of information there. You can verify anything from money supplies to oil production to GDP rates to inflation rates … etc. For example:

01. http://www.tradingeconomics.com
Iraq's money supply

02. http://www.tradingeconomics.com/iraq/money-supply-m0

China's money supply

03. http://www.tradingeconomics.com/china/money-supply-m2

04. http://www.bloomberg.com/news/2013-08-01/china-s-real-exchange-rate-undervalued-5-10-imf-report-says.html

05. http://www.tradingeconomics.com/china/foreign-exchange-reserves

Here are some links that reveal Vietnam's money supply

06. http://www.tradingeconomics.com/vietnam/money-supply-m2

07. http://www.vietnamtravel.org/money

Here is a great search engine for economic data

08. https://www.quandl.com/

There are other good sites available to verify the numbers in this book. Look at these sites for gold supplies

09. http://www.tradingeconomics.com/china/gold-reserves

10. http://demonocracy.info/infographics/world/gold/gold.html

11. http://en.wikipedia.org/wiki/Gold_reserve#Officially_reported_gold_holdings

12. http://www.imf.org/external/np/sta/ir/IRProcessWeb/colist.aspx

13. http://www.mining-technology.com/features/feature-the-10-biggest-silver-mines-in-the-world/

America's Money supply

14. http://www.federalreserve.gov/faqs/currency_12770.htm

15. http://www.tradingeconomics.com/united-states/money-supply-m0

The Petrodollar System also known as The U.S.-Saudi Arabian Joint Commission on Economic Cooperation.

16. http://www.investopedia.com/articles/forex/072915/how-petrodollars-affect-us-dollar.asp

17. http://faculty.georgetown.edu/imo3/petrod/petro2.htm

18. https://en.wikipedia.org/wiki/Nixon_shock

19. http://www.history.com/this-day-in-history/fdr-takes-united-states-off-gold-standard

20. http://www.gao.gov/products/ID-79-7

PIIGS

21. http://demonocracy.info/infographics/eu/debt_piigs/debt_piigs.html

Many sites can back up the things that I wrote about NESARA. Wikipedia has a few good sites. Here are a few links to get you started.

22. http://www.nesarasucks.com/
23. http://en.wikipedia.org/wiki/Omega_Trust
24. http://en.wikipedia.org/wiki/NESARA
25. http://en.wikipedia.org/wiki/J._Z._Knight#Ramtha

Read the book that the Federal Reserve put out called Modern Money Mechanics. This explains Fractional Reserve Banking in detail. Read more links that debunk the Federal Reserve conspiracies and the income tax laws

26. https://archive.org/details/ModernMoneyMechanics
27. http://skepticproject.com/articles/zeitgeist/part-three/#ig_farben_and_others
28. http://www.federalreservehistory.org/Events/DetailView/10
29. https://www.federalreserveeducation.org/about-the-fed/history
30. https://fee.org/articles/gold-policy-in-the-1930s/
31. https://www.congress.gov/bill/93rd-congress/senate-bill/02665
32. http://www.usconstitution.net/constamrat.html#Am16
33. http://docs.law.gwu.edu/facweb/jsiegel/Personal/taxes/JustNoLaw.htm

Here are links that explain why the dollar remains the world's currency reserve

34. http://economix.blogs.nytimes.com/2014/03/26/qa-why-the-dollar-remains-the-reserve-currency/?_php=true&_type=blogs&_r=0
35. http://www.federalist-debate.org/index.php/component/k2/item/115-the-debate-about-the-sdr-as-a-global-reserve-currency-and-sdr-denominated-securities
36. http://www.forbes.com/sites/billconerly/2013/10/25/future-of-the-dollar-as-world-reserve-currency/
37. http://www.investopedia.com/articles/investing/090715/us-will-remain-worlds-reserve-currency.asp

38. http://www.nytimes.com/2012/04/25/world/africa/using-us-dollars-zimbabwe-finds-a-problem-no-change.html?_r=1&

39. http://www.zerohedge.com/article/history-worlds-reserve-currency-ancient-greece-today

40. http://www.investopedia.com/articles/forex/040915/countries-use-us-dollar.asp

Here are some great links to help verify what I said about the dinar

41. http://content.time.com/time/magazine/article/0,9171,998512,00.html

42. http://www.rferl.org/content/article/1095057.html

43. http://www.rferl.org/content/iraq_said_planning_currency_overhaul_redenomination/24245867.html

44. http://www.alsumaria.tv/news/43253/iraqs-central-bank-to-delete-zeros-from-iraqi-curr

45. http://articles.latimes.com/keyword/kuwait-currency

46. http://www.nytimes.com/1991/03/25/world/after-the-war-no-electricity-but-kuwait-reopens-its-banks.html

47. http://articles.latimes.com/1991-03-24/news/mn-1395_1_kuwaiti-banks

48. http://www.cbi.iq/documents/CBILAW-EN_f.pdf

49. http://www.cftc.gov/opa/enf98/opaforexa15.htm

50. http://dfi.wa.gov/consumers/alerts/iraqi-dinar-scams.htm

51. http://www.ice.gov/news/releases/south-dakota-man-pleads-guilty-evading-reporting-requirements-importing-foreign

52. http://www.realscam.com/attachments/f12/1576d1348185792-bayshore-capital-investments-bh-group-bhgroup_indictment.pdf

53. http://sd.findacase.com/research/wfrmDocViewer.aspx/xq/fac.20120906_0000116.DSD.htm/qx

54. http://www.nytimes.com/1993/05/16/world/fortunes-in-iraqi-bills-gone-overnight.html?src=pm

55. http://people.ischool.berkeley.edu/~hal/people/hal/NYTimes/2004-01-15.html

56. http://jpkoning.blogspot.com/2013/05/disowned-currency-odd-case-of-iraqi.html

57. http://www.bostonfed.org/economic/ppdp/2004/ppdp0401.pdf

58. http://www.pigottlaw.com/Iraqi-Dinar-Scam

59. http://www.unc.edu/~lmosley/APSA%202005.pdf

60. https://iraqcurrencywatch.com/

Keynesian Economics

61. https://fee.org/articles/you-never-go-full-keynesian/

62. https://danieljmitchell.wordpress.com/2009/04/10/keynesian-economics-is-wrong/

There are a lot of conspiracy sites on the internet that rewrite history and make up quotes from our Founding Fathers. These are mainly blog sites and other personal websites. A quote from a president or founding father must be verified, and it is easy to do this. The following sites verify these quotes and American history.

63. http://www.revolutionary-war-and-beyond.com/american-historical-documents.html

64. http://oll.libertyfund.org/
65. https://docs.google.com/file/d/13QFCM4HA_gFGe_F9lzfMTzpGuikBZ4Zg70ahJDp6YMFzjTDuSajXOHgUrpt_/edit?pli=1
66. http://www.sjsu.edu/faculty/watkins/BofUS.htm
67. http://www.buyandhold.com/bh/en/education/history/2000/122499.html
68. https://www.jpmorgan.com/pages/jpmorgan/about/history/month/oct
69. http://tjrs.monticello.org/archive/search/quotes
70. http://en.wikipedia.org/wiki/Large_denominations_of_United_States_currency
71. http://www.moneyfactory.gov/uscurrency.html

It is easy to debase a currency by printing more of it. How do exchange rates affect imports and exports, and why do countries want a low exchange rate to strengthen their exports? Check these links.

72. http://www.econedlink.org/lessons/index.php?lid=342&type=student
74. http://www.econedlink.org/lessons/projector.php?lid=342&type=educator
75. http://www.amosweb.com/cgi-bin/awb_nav.pl?s=wpd&c=dsp&k=exchange+rates,+aggregate+demand+determinant
76. http://www.investopedia.com/articles/basics/04/050704.asp
77. http://education-portal.com/academy/lesson/how-currency-

changes-affect-imports-and-exports.html#transcript'
   China's cancer villages
   78. http://www.bbc.com/news/world-asia-china-21545868
   79. http://www.environmentmagazine.org/Archives/Back%20Issues/March-April%202010/made-in-china-full.html
   80. https://www.google.com/maps/d/viewer?mid=zoltdQ3AnjHQ.kJGsxnMyxV3c&msa=0
   Gold and silver is used in the manufacturing of electronics.
   81. https://www.youtube.com/watch?v=uEErWlpZNlQ
   82. http://www.numbersleuth.org/worlds-gold/ More information about gold
   83. https://www.youtube.com/watch?v=r2_zHO2Neas&t=0s
   84. https://www.gold.org/about-us
   85. http://www.coinnews.net/mints/edmund-c-moy-director-of-united-states-mint-biography-speeches-and-statements/
   86. http://www.newsmax.com/Finance/Ed-Moy/Fort-Knox-gold-bar-audit/2014/06/06/id/575519
   87. https://en.wikipedia.org/wiki/Gold_repatriation
   Here is some information regarding the end of BRICS
   88. http://www.telegraph.co.uk/business/2016/03/06/downfall-of-brazils-lula-marks-end-of-brics-fantasy/
   89. http://time.com/4106094/goldman-sachs-brics/

90. http://www.forbes.com/sites/panosmourdoukoutas/2016/03/07/where-did-chinas-half-a-trillion-u-s-dollars-reserves-go/#34fd43654675

There are 90 links to get you started. Check the data in this book against those links and spend some time doing your own research. You will soon see the hype involved in the conspiracy theory called The Global Currency Reset.

Videos I made

91 https://www.youtube.com/watch?v=D3WedTO3pQU&t=0s

Here are some more links that cover the reason for the 2008 meltdown. You can see that the government played a major role in the global meltdown.

92. https://www.youtube.com/watch?v=cMnSp4qEXNM

93. http://www.theatlantic.com/business/archive/2011/12/hey-barney-frank-the-government-did-cause-the-housing-crisis/249903/

94. https://www.aei.org/publication/the-error-at-the-heart-of-the-dodd-frank-act/

95. http://www.ecominoes.com/2012/05/frank-and-dodd-started-mortgage-crisis.html

96. http://www.aei.org/publication/illegitimate-dodd-frank-law-nothing-financial-crisis/

I would like to thank you for downloading and reading this eBook. Hopefully it can be used as a source to verify economic principles, and it will address the fears that people feel when they fall for many of these conspiracy theories. That is the ultimate goal and purpose for writing it!

About The Author

Marcus Curtis has worked for a Fortune 500 company for over 25 years. He has a diversified portfolio, including investments in the stock market and precious metals. He has spent seven years studying economics, beginning his studies in 2009 shortly after the 2008 melt down.

Marcus owned Iraqi dinar for a brief period of time starting in 2010, but sold all of it back to a dealer shortly after discovering that it was a scam. He operates a popular blog website that is dedicated to educating people trapped in the dinar scam called Iraq Currency Watch. You will find many podcasts and videos about some of the content covered in this book, along with some basic economic information

https://iraqcurrencywatch.com/

Because many economic scams are targeted at Christians, Marcus also operates another website that explains basic economics within a biblical context. This site is part of an ongoing work. It is called Biblical Views and World Economics.

https://bvawe.wordpress.com/

Marcus is also a musician. He plays guitar, bass, and drums. He has studied a variety of musical styles including classical, blues, jazz, ragtime, contemporary acoustic, metal, rock, and hard rock.

He has also worked in several recording studios, and today he operates his own home studio. He has done engineering work for musicians in the Tulsa area, and was a member of the Tulsa Guitar Society. Within the past few years he has produced CDs for society members. The Tulsa Guitar Society has recently disbanded. He has written another book that reveals tips about marketing yourself as a musician. This book describes many ways that a musician can set up multiple streams of income.

https://www.amazon.in/Business-Music-Musicians-Recording-Marketing-ebook/dp/B00YVE4X2C

http://www.marcuscurtismusic.com/

https://www.reverbnation.com/marcuscurtis

Made in the USA
Columbia, SC
09 January 2020